All the
very best
we are proud of you
Michael Levine

NOT MANY PEOPLE
KNOW THAT!

Royalties to the National
Playing Fields Association

NOT MANY PEOPLE KNOW THAT!

Michael Caine's

Almanac of Amazing Information

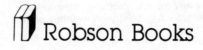 Robson Books

Illustrations by JOHN JENSEN

FIRST PUBLISHED IN GREAT BRITAIN IN 1984 BY
ROBSON BOOKS LTD., BOLSOVER HOUSE, 5–6
CLIPSTONE STREET, LONDON W1P 7EB. TEXT
COPYRIGHT © 1984 MICHAEL CAINE. ILLUSTRATIONS
COPYRIGHT © 1984 JOHN JENSEN.

First impression October 1984
Second impression November 1984
Third impression November 1984
Fourth impression December 1984

British Library Cataloguing in Publication Data
Caine, Michael
    Not many people know that.
    1. Encyclopedias and dictionaries
    I. Title
    032'.02   AE6

ISBN 0-86051-298-3

Printed and bound in Great Britain by
Biddles Ltd, Guildford and King's Lynn

Introduction

If you turn to March you'll see that Einstein and I have the same birthday. You could also say we share a sense of inquisitiveness. Some would say it's written in the stars; we're both Pisceans. Only Einstein wasn't born a Cockney, and maths was never my strong point. His interests took him on to change the course of science. Mine led me to find out all I could about the odd things in life.

I was three and a half years old when I made the first discovery that's stuck with me. A piano tuner came to sort out the piano at my infant school and I remember being fascinated that he had a white stick. I couldn't understand why a blind man had been given the job. I suppose I was too timid at that age to ask him outright, so one of the teachers explained that his blindness was an asset. With one of his senses gone, the others were keener than ever. He had a finer touch and a far sharper ear than any sighted person. I was amazed. Not many three and a half year-olds knew that.

As I grew older, that sort of quick-witted, Cockney knowledge helped me earn my place in the gang around the Elephant and Castle where I played.

Being an actor helps too. Ten years of occasional work and long periods of enforced 'resting' gave me time to read and read. Ever since I learned the alphabet I've been intrigued by words. Evacuated as a kid in Norfolk, or at home in London, in Southwark Public Library, books were welcome companions. (At school I was known as the Professor because I spent so much time reading.) As an actor I've been able to develop an already retentive memory, and mine's been hoarding nuggets of information now for nearly half a century.

There's another side to this magpie collection of odd facts. It's a wonderful way to deflate stuffed-shirts and pop over-inflated egos. There's nothing like a well-timed fact to take the wind from a know-all's sails.

It's entertaining too; or it should be. In the film of 'The Wrong Box', I played a shy medical student in specs, who was secretly admiring the girl next door. She was played by Nanette Newman, whose uncle, played by Sir Ralph Richardson, had spent his life picking up pieces of amazing information. His problem was he didn't know when to stop and he ended up boring everyone silly as he chuntered on from one revelation to the next. I hope I'm different. I like to use my facts sparingly.

The trouble is there's not a lot you can say after being told that Marie Antoinette and Jayne Mansfield had the same bust measurement, or that a spider has its penis on the end of one of its legs. It was Peter Sellers who pointed out that I always followed up these facts with what has become my catch-phrase and is the title of this book. I never realized this until Peter impersonated me for the first time. Finding out something like that about yourself comes as quite a shock.

As it happens, I could mimick him pretty well too. It was my voice that answered calls on Peter Sellers's answerphone.

Now, not many people know that!

Michael Caine

August, 1984

P.S. This book is being published in aid of the National Playing Fields Association which celebrates its Diamond Jubilee in 1985. If you want to know more about the charity and its important work, turn to page 223.

JANUARY

John Paul Getty, once the richest man in the world, had a payphone in his huge mansion.

On the night of 22-23 January 1879, a detachment of the South Wales Borderers and a handful of Royal Engineers fought off wave after wave of Zulu warriors in the defence of Rorkes Drift in South Africa. They set a record by winning eleven VC's before breakfast in that action, and also gave me the biggest break of my career in 'Zulu' eighty-four years later.

I thought I'd done my homework thoroughly for this film. I'd even found a photograph of the original Gonville Bromhead, who I played, and discovered that we weren't exactly identical twins. He was dark, five-foot-six and with a black beard. After the première, however, one of his fifty or so descendants, who'd come to the screening, politely took me aside to say: 'The name's Brumhead – not Bromhead.'

You can't win them all!

JANUARY (1)

Idi Amin, later to become one of the most ruthless tyrants the world has ever seen, was born on 1 January 1928. Before the coup which brought him to power, Amin served in the British Army, and was a noted Rugby player.

Nineteenth-century artist, Cesar Ducornet, drew with his feet — he didn't have any arms.

John Paul Getty, once the richest man in the world, had a payphone in his huge mansion.

The original cost of 'spending a penny' in the first public toilets installed in England in 1852, was tuppence.

George Washington grew marijuana in his garden.

JANUARY (2)

One of Britain's most famous composers was born today in 1905. Sir Michael Tippett's pieces are notoriously difficult to play. For instance, at the première of his 'Symphony No. 2', the orchestra got lost in the middle of the piece and the conductor had to go back to the beginning and start again.

Chop-suey is not a native Chinese dish. It was, invented by Chinese immigrants in California.

The average human brain weighs three pounds.

The Hundred Years' War lasted 116 years.

The Islands of Langerhans are not a holiday resort, but a group of cells situated in the pancreas.

JANUARY 3

On 3 January 1892, J.R.R. Tolkien was born. His famous book, **Lord of the Rings**, has sold over three million copies and has been translated into nine languages. Writing was not his original profession, however — he was Professor of Literature at Oxford University.

The sun's mass decreases by four million tons per second.

An elephant has the world's largest penis. It weighs on average sixty pounds.

Judy Garland's false eyelashes were sold at auction in 1979 for US $125.

Albert Einstein was once offered the Presidency of Israel. He refused saying he had no head for problems.

JANUARY 4

The famous midget, 'General Tom Thumb', was born on this day back in 1838. Though he came from a normal family, he stopped growing at the age of six months, and was signed up by the circus owner, P.T. Barnum, when he was only five. Courted by celebrities and royalty, his eventual adult height was a mere forty inches.

Greenland is the largest island in the world. It is about ten times the size of the whole of Great Britain.

Gerald Ford, who became President of the US after the resignation of Richard Nixon, was a male model before he went into politics.

The correct name for a group of crows is a 'murder'.

Karl Marx disapproved of Engels' mistress because she was too common.

JANUARY (5)

For Roman Catholics, 5 January is St Simeon Stylites' Day. He was a fifth-century hermit who showed his total devotion to God by spending literally years sitting on top of a huge flagpole.

Joe Davis, former world champion Snooker player, only had one good eye.

According to aeronautical science, the bumble-bee shouldn't be able to fly.

Worms are hermaphroditic — they have both sets of sexual organs on their bodies.

France gave women the vote only in 1944.

JANUARY (6)

Richard II was born today in 1367. When he died in 1400, a hole was left in the side of his tomb so that people could touch his royal head. In 1776, things got out of hand and someone reached in and stole his jawbone.

The Guinness Book of Records has broken a record of its own — it is the book which is most often stolen from British Public Libraries.

There are more bacteria in a hospital operating theatre than there are in an ordinary living-room.

A Korean child called Kim could speak four languages and do advanced calculus by the time he was five years old.

In the original story, Cinderella's slippers were made of fur. The idea that they were glass arose from a mistake during translation.

JANUARY (7)

On 7 January 1904, the 'CQD' distress signal was officially introduced, 'CQ' standing for 'Seek You' with a 'D' for 'Danger' added. It only lasted for a couple of years before the now-familiar 'SOS' signal took over in 1906.

Catherine de Medici drilled a hole in her bedroom floor so that she could see her husband making love to his mistress in the room below.

Sir Winston Churchill wrote a number of film scripts.

The leading part in Shakespeare's **The Merchant of Venice** is Shylock the Jew, though the play was written at a time when Jews were banned from living in Britain.

John Glenn, the American astronaut who carried out the first manned orbit of the earth, was showered with 3,474 tons of ticker-tape when he got back.

JANUARY (8)

On 8 January 1935, Elvis 'The Pelvis' Presley came into the world. His impact on modern music is immeasurable and, though his records are still selling, it is estimated that he has received over eighty gold discs (one million sales) worldwide.

If you got rid of all the space in the atoms which go to make up a camel, you **could** pass a camel through the eye of a needle.

Seventh-century Mexican natives, the Toltecs, went into battle with wooden swords so as not to kill their enemies.

During World War Two, W.C. Fields kept US $50,000 in Hitler's Germany 'in case the little bastard wins'.

Henry VII was the only British King ever crowned on the field of battle.

JANUARY (9)

Richard Nixon, disgraced US President, was born today in 1913. His career in politics began after he answered an advertisement asking for a Republican candidate for Congress in 1946. Nixon had no previous experience of politics, but was able to overturn a huge Democrat majority largely by labelling his rival a 'closet' Communist. He never looked back.

The amount of carbon in the human body is enough to fill about nine thousand lead pencils.

The Forth railway bridge in Scotland is a metre longer in the summer than in the winter.

Pope Adrian VI died after a fly got stuck in his throat as he was taking a drink from a water fountain.

King Solomon of Israel had some seven hundred wives, as well as hundreds of mistresses.

JANUARY (10)

Frank James, brother of Jesse James, and member of the infamous James Gang, was born on 10 January 1843. He saw himself as a bit of an intellectual, and was always ready to quote Shakespeare when the occasion demanded. When he was caught, his trial attracted such public interest that it had to be moved from the local county court to the opera house to accommodate everybody.

Turkey has put a ban on people kissing in films.

Franklin D. Roosevelt, the only US President to be elected three times, had polio.

People in the East used to believe that powdered rhinoceros horn could increase their sexual potency.

The song which is sung most often in the world — 'Happy Birthday To You' — is still under copyright. It runs out in 2010.

JANUARY (11)

Thomas Hardy, the English poet and novelist, died on 11 January 1928. Because of his fame, his ashes were buried in Westminster Abbey, but his heart was removed and placed in the grave of his beloved first wife in Stinsford Churchyard.

The 'Mona Lisa' was originally bought by Francis I of France in 1517 to hang in his bathroom. The painting is now valued at over £35 million.

In 1901, Dr Dussaud demonstrated his latest invention — a cinematograph for the blind. Unfortunately it didn't catch on.

Handel wrote the score of his Messiah in just over three weeks.

Charles Sauson inherited the post of official executioner from his father in 1726, at the tender age of seven.

JANUARY (12)

On 12 January 1948, the first full-size supermarket to be built in Britain received its grand opening. It was called 'The London Co-op' at Manor Park.

Frederick William of Prussia sent his agents all over Europe to recruit a crack army of men who were at least six feet tall. The army was eventually organized, but its members were never able to show their worth as they never fired a shot in anger.

In winter, the skating rinks in the parks of Moscow cover more than 250,000 square metres of land.

It was the custom in Ancient Rome for the men to place their right hand on their testicles when taking an oath. The modern word 'testimony' is derived from this old tradition.

The hydrochloric acid in the human digestive system is strong enough to dissolve a nail.

JANUARY (13)

James Joyce died from a perforated duodenal ulcer on this day in 1941. Many people find his later work very difficult to read, in spite of its enormous critical acclaim. Ironically, his last words are reported to have been: 'Does nobody understand?'

The Marx Brothers (Chico, Harpo, Groucho, and Zeppo) were actually named respectively Leonard, Adolph, Julius, and Herbert.

The background radiation in Aberdeen is twice that of the rest of Great Britain.

The Spanish Inquisition once condemned the whole of The Netherlands to death for heresy.

Ethelred the Unready, King of England in the tenth century, was found on his wedding night in bed with both his wife **and** his mother-in-law.

JANUARY (14)

When Humphrey Bogart died on 14 January 1957, his wife Lauren Bacall placed a gold whistle inside his coffin. The inscription on the whistle read: 'If you need anything, just whistle', which is a line from their first film together 'To Have and Have Not'.

Giotto became the official Vatican artist after he impressed Pope Benedict XI by drawing a perfect circle with his paintbrush, completely freehand.

Lewis Carroll is said to have had a penchant for photographing little girls in the nude.

The Great Pyramid of Cheops in Egypt is large enough to enclose the main cathedrals of Milan, Florence, Rome, and London.

Turtles, as a species, are about 275 million years old.

JANUARY (15)

On this day in 1867, there was a severe frost in London. However, over forty people died when the ice broke on the main lake in Regent's Park.

Bob Hope, before he became a world famous comedian, was a boxer.

The Angel Falls in Venezuela are nearly twenty times taller than the Niagara Falls.

José Olmedo, the Ecuadorian poet, has a statue in his honour in his home country. Because of limited funds, the government decided not to commission a sculptor to do the job; instead they bought a second-hand statue of the English poet Lord Byron.

Three-fifths of all species of mammals are rodents.

JANUARY (16)

Prohibition began on 16 January 1920 in the US, and so, almost inevitably, did the practice of bootlegging. Bootlegging got its name from the cowboys' old method of hiding alcohol in their boots when selling it illegally to the Indians in the previous century.

There are about ten times as many sheep in Australia as human beings.

In 1935, Jesse Owens broke four world records in the space of forty-five minutes.

The phrase 'The Three Rs', standing for 'reading, writing, and arithmetic', was coined by Sir William Curtis, who was illiterate.

JANUARY (17)

Benjamin Franklin, one of America's most loved heroes, who helped to write the 'Declaration of Independence', was born on this day in 1706. It must not be forgotten that one of his greatest achievements was the invention of the rocking-chair.

George Bernard Shaw refused an Oscar for the screenplay of **Pygmalion** in 1938.

About two-thirds of the world's population do not come into regular contact with newspapers, television, radio, or telephone.

An elephant's trunk can hold one-and-a-half gallons of water.

The Earth, for its size, has the largest satellite of any planet in the Solar System — the Moon.

JANUARY (18)

Cary Grant, one of Hollywood's most successful actors, was born in Bristol, England on 18 January 1904. He was notorious for being evasive about his true age. When a journalist sent him a telegram asking: 'How old Cary Grant?', he replied with another saying: 'Old Cary Grant fine. How you?'

'The' is the most used word in the English language, followed by 'of' and 'and'.

The only vaguely feline thing in Dick Whittington's life was his highly successful trading ship, **The Cat**.

The 1970 World Cup football match between El Salvador and Honduras was so highly charged that it resulted in the two countries embarking on a three-day war.

JANUARY 19

James Watt, who perfected the idea of the steam engine, was born today in 1736. He suffered severe migraines throughout his life.

Oxygen molecules travel at roughly the same speed as a jet aircraft.

William Gladstone, who was Liberal Prime Minister four times during his long Parliamentary career, was initially a Tory Chancellor of the Exchequer.

When his first steamer arrived in Boston in 1890, Mr Cunard, the owner, received around two thousand invitations to dinner, such was the interest aroused. If he had accepted them all, he would have been able to dine out every night for five-and-a-half years.

Only female mosquitoes bite.

JANUARY 20

Oil magnate, Aristotle Onassis, was born on this day in 1906. A multi-millionaire, with many oil tankers, he once got involved in what amounted to a private war with Peru.

The most common surname in France is 'Martin'.

Walt Disney himself did the original voice for the cartoon character, Mickey Mouse.

St Nicholas, the original Father Christmas, is patron saint of thieves, virgins, and communist Russia.

A shark has to keep moving forward in order to live.

JANUARY (21)

Lenin, the great Russian leader, died on this day in 1924. He suffered from a brain illness late in his life and, by the time of his death, his brain was a quarter of its normal size. Apparently, he spent his declining years collecting mushrooms.

Some parts of Paris have public flush toilets for dogs.

A Muslim can divorce any of his wives by simply repeating the phrase 'I divorce you' three times in her company.

A greenfly born on a Sunday can become a grandparent by the following Wednesday.

In the 1970s, the Rhode Island Legislature in the US entertained a proposal that there be a two dollar tax on every act of sexual intercourse in the State.

JANUARY (22)

Queen Victoria died on 22 January 1901. Among her many claims to fame, she was the first person ever to use chloroform to combat the pain of childbirth.

Some Indian fakirs claim to have lain on a bed of nails for over one hundred days, although such feats have never been fully substantiated.

There is no mention of cats in the Bible.

The amount spent on advertising Coca-Cola over the years is equivalent to providing every family in the world with one free bottle.

Tallulah Bankhead once claimed that she was as 'pure as the driven slush'.

JANUARY (23)

Humphrey Bogart was born today in 1899, although his film company, Warner Brothers, claimed that he was born on Christmas Day in order to romanticize his image.

Some Eskimos use refrigerators to keep their food from freezing.

Your body contains enough iron to make a spike strong enough to hold your weight.

A chicken in New Zealand once laid three hundred and sixty-one eggs in the space of one calendar year.

The city of Istanbul straddles two separate continents — Europe and Asia.

JANUARY (24)

Frederick the Great, King of Prussia, was born on 24 January 1712. He became a great military commander, as well as something of an eccentric. For example, he often had his coffee made with Champagne instead of water.

One of Queen Victoria's wedding gifts was a half-ton cheese, which was over nine feet in diameter.

The novelist, Anthony Burgess, admits to having been in a state of 'near drunkenness' while he was writing **A Clockwork Orange**, because he found the material so depressing. Much of it is based on his own experiences, though the novel is set in the future.

The average person has fewer than two legs.

According to an old English system of time units, a moment is defined as lasting one-and-a-half minutes.

JANUARY (25)

On this day in 1882, the novelist Virginia Woolf was born. Strangely, she wrote a lot of her work standing up.

The 'Over The Rainbow' scene from 'The Wizard of Oz' was originally cut from the final film because the producers thought it too slow, and contributed little to the plot. It was only restored at the last minute.

Catgut does not come from cats, but is made from the intestines of sheep.

David Renwick of Sheffield, England, makes iron chastity belts to order.

Ice is lighter than water.

JANUARY (26)

On this day back in 1905, Captain Wells discovered the famous 'Cullinan' diamond at the Premier mine in South Africa. It still ranks as the largest diamond ever found in the world, weighing over one-and-a-quarter pounds.

Adolf Eichmann (head of the Jewish Office at the Gestapo, and responsible for countless deaths during World War Two) was originally a travelling salesman for the Vacuum Oil Co. of Austria.

Crocodiles are colour-blind.

It would take about two million hydrogen atoms to cover the average-sized full stop.

JANUARY (27)

Charles Dodgson, better known as Lewis Carroll, author of **Alice's Adventures in Wonderland**, was born today in 1832. He claimed that he wrote 98,721 letters in the last thirty-seven years of his life. That is an average of over seven letters a day.

To make just one pound of honey, bees must collect nectar from over two million separate flowers.

The Dutch Army is unionized.

According to Marco Polo, the Chinese ruler Kublai Khan had over five thousand astrologers at his court. They were used for such things as weather prediction, and there were severe penalties for any mistakes.

Not all dinosaurs were huge and frightening; in fact, some were as small as chickens.

JANUARY (28)

Henry VIII, perhaps the most famous English King of all, died on 28 January 1547. He is well-known for having had six wives, and it seems appropriate that his armour has the largest codpiece in the Tower of London.

Cats have no facility for tasting sugar.

In 1849, David Atchison became President of the US for just one day, and he spent most of the day asleep.

There are two miles of passages in The Houses of Parliament.

Nutmeg, if injected intravenously, is fatal.

JANUARY (29)

King George III died today in 1820. As the years progressed, his mental state deteriorated badly, and he was finally acknowledged to be violently insane in 1811.

The eye of a giant squid is larger than a person's head.

The US has a marriage bureau to help find suitable partners for lonely cats and dogs.

The study of stupidity is called morology.

The biggest fish and chip shop in the world is Harry Ramsden's in Yorkshire.

JANUARY (30)

Gandhi was assassinated on 30 January 1948. The fanatical Hindu assassin first gave Gandhi the traditional religious greeting, and then shot him several times at point-blank range. As he was dying, Gandhi turned to his murderer and gave him the Hindu sign of forgiveness.

The two highest IQs ever recorded (on a standard test) both belonged to women.

Australian earthworms can grow up to ten feet in length.

The ordinary house-fly beats its wings nearly two hundred times a second.

In The Andes, time is often measured by how long it takes to smoke a cigarette.

JANUARY (31)

Franz Schubert, the composer, was born on this day in 1797. He was a very poor man, and many of his compositions were first tried out over a drink with friends in his local tavern.

Over two thousand pints of beer are drunk in the House of Commons every week.

In many juke-boxes you can actually buy recorded silence.

Dolphins sleep with one eye open.

Biscuits get their name from two French words, 'bis cuit', which mean 'twice cooked'. The original biscuits had to be preserved for long periods and had to be cooked twice to make them last as long as possible.

FEBRUARY

Snails can sleep for three years without waking up.

Clark Gable (born 1 February) and Humphrey Bogart, an idol of my film-going days at school and the actor who taught me the importance of not blinking or moving my eyes in close-ups, had originally been lined up for John Huston's film version of Rudyard Kipling's story 'The Man Who Would Be King'.

When the film was finally made in 1975 I took the part of Peachy Carnehan, originally assigned to Bogie, and Sean Connery played Daniel Dravot, the part that Clark Gable was to have when Huston first came up with the idea.

Filming was murder. Sean and I are old friends and together are two of the worst corpsers in the business. Dressed up as an Indian beggar and later a self-styled king complete with crown, he nearly had me in tears of laughter in many of the scenes.

To make it even more of a 'family' affair, Christopher Plummer – who'd played Hamlet in my one brush with the Bard – took the part of Kipling himself. And Shakira, my wife, played the mysterious Princess Roxanne – and has vowed to stay clear of film work ever since!

FEBRUARY (1)

The film-star, Clark Gable, was born today in 1901. He received a medal for a series of courageous bomber missions during World War Two, and reached the rank of Major.

You have to frown nearly a quarter of a million times to make one wrinkle.

Rats can't vomit.

South American gauchos sometimes put raw steaks under their saddles before starting a day's riding, in order to tenderize the meat.

Snails can sleep for three years without waking up.

FEBRUARY (2)

On 2 February 1918, John L. Sullivan, a famous bareknuckle boxer, died. His fights usually carried on until one man or the other collapsed, either from an over liberal use of alcohol between rounds, or from exhaustion. He once knocked out an opponent, Jake Kilrain, in the seventy-fifth round.

Kangaroos are only one inch long at birth.

Although Cleopatra was meant to have died after a bite from an asp, the species does not exist in Egypt.

You are not allowed to play tennis on the streets of Cambridge.

Colour televisions only produce three colours.

FEBRUARY 3

Elizabeth Blackwell, who was born in Bristol, England, on 3 February 1821, was the first woman in America to gain an M.D. degree.

Henry VIII, though he had been excommunicated from the church for his many divorces, still retained the title of 'Defender of the Faith', which the Pope had given him many years earlier for an article attacking Martin Luther.

Sir Winston Churchill was born in a ladies' cloakroom, after his mother went into labour during a dance at Blenheim Palace.

The 'Crystal Palace', at the Great Exhibition of 1851, which contained one million square feet of glass, was visited by over six million people.

The English language contains about 490,000 words (excluding some 300,000 technical terms).

FEBRUARY 4

This day in 1962 was a Sunday, and saw the appearance of the first-ever colour magazine supplement. It was produced by the **Sunday Times**.

There is a piece of string in America which weighs about ten thousand pounds.

It has been estimated that a normal paper parking-ticket will, on average, disintegrate in under four weeks.

In the seventeenth century, a Boston man was sentenced to two hours in the stocks for obscene behaviour. His only crime was to kiss his wife in public on a Sunday.

Half of the world's area of land water is in Canada.

FEBRUARY 5

Sir Robert Peel, who was born on this day in 1788, was the founder of the Metropolitan Police Force in London. Originally known as 'Peel's Bloody Gang', his name is more kindly remembered in the nickname commonly given to police constables, 'bobbies'.

An albatross can stay airborne without flapping its wings for days on end.

The original title for the best-selling book, **Gone With The Wind**, was **Ba! Ba! Black Sheep**.

The Sun makes up over ninety-nine per cent of the Solar System's weight.

Tokyo has a restaurant for dogs.

FEBRUARY 6

Queen Elizabeth II came to the Throne today back in 1952, after the death of her father George VI. Many important world figures are entertained at Buckingham Palace each year, and a ruler is used to position place-settings at meals.

Whales can't swim backwards.

After the first moon walk, Pan-American Airlines announced that they were willing to take enquiries about future commercial flights to the moon. They received eighty thousand requests immediately.

Eighteen of Britain's forty-six Prime Ministers have been Old Etonians.

Fifty-pence coins have a life expectancy of around fifty years.

FEBRUARY 7

On this day in 1837, Florence Nightingale claimed she had a vision of God. God told her to renounce her rich social background, and take up a mission in life. A few years later she took up nursing.

One gallon of fuel moves the **QE2** six inches.

Two minor earthquakes occur every minute somewhere in the world.

The average British family uses two miles of toilet paper a year.

The perilous journey undertaken by the human sperm prior to conception, could be compared to someone swimming in treacle the distance across the Atlantic Ocean.

FEBRUARY 8

John Ruskin, the art critic, was born on 8 February 1819. He records that he was so shocked by the sight of his wife's pubic hair when he viewed it for the first time on their wedding night, that the marriage was never consummated.

The surface area of one human lung is equal to that of a tennis court.

An octopus has three hearts.

Every British Post Office is given a small grant towards the upkeep of a cat. They are meant to be used as mice-catchers.

Every pint of water taken from the Red Sea would contain four ounces of salt.

FEBRUARY 9

On 9 February 1942, soap rationing began in Britain.

Since 1959, more than six thousand pieces of space machinery have fallen out of orbit — many of these have hit the earth's surface.

Gorgias of Epirus was born during the funeral of his mother.

The longest kiss in the history of Hollywood came in the 1941 film, 'You're in the Army Now'. Reg Toomey and Jane Wyman were locked together for three minutes and five seconds.

Thomas Carlyle, the English historian, was forced to become left-handed, after he had the misfortune of losing his right hand.

FEBRUARY 10

The American swimmer, Mark Spitz, was born on this day in 1950. In the 1972 Olympics, he won four individual gold medals, and was a member of three winning relay-teams. All seven of his victories also resulted in world records.

An American aircraft in Vietnam shot itself down with one of its own missiles.

Some soft drinks are made sweeter by adding coal.

You use forty-three muscles to frown, and only seventeen to smile.

Sophia Loren's sister was once married to the son of Italian dictator, Mussolini.

FEBRUARY (11)

Peasant girl Bernadette Soubirous was born today in 1858. When she was fourteen years old, she had a vision of the Virgin Mary at a grotto near Lourdes in France. The town is now one of the most popular places for pilgrimage in the world, and Bernadette has become a Saint.

Because metal was scarce, the Oscars given out during World War Two were made of wood.

In Ancient China, people committed suicide by consuming a pound of salt.

Dogs sweat through the pads of their feet.

The Puritans forbade the singing of Christmas Carols, judging them to be out of keeping with the true spirit of Christmas.

FEBRUARY (12)

Abraham Lincoln was born today in 1809. During the American Civil War, the King of Siam offered him the use of his official war elephants. Lincoln declined the offer.

Some people believe that chewing gum while peeling an onion will prevent you from shedding any tears.

The author of **Gulliver's Travels**, Jonathan Swift, once took a vow of silence for a whole year.

Only two words in the English language end in the letters 'shion' — 'cushion' and 'fashion'.

During the reign of Elizabeth I, there was a tax put on men's beards.

FEBRUARY 13

Georges Simenon, the prolific French writer, was born on 13 February 1903. He wrote under seventeen different pseudonyms, and produced over five hundred novels in his lifetime, many of them dealing with his famous detective, Inspector Maigret. He once claimed to have written a regular eighty pages in the four hours before breakfast each morning.

People in Siberia usually buy their milk frozen on a stick.

On average, we all contain two molecules of Julius Caesar's last breath.

The State flag of Alaska was designed by a thirteen-year-old boy.

The Kiwi is the only bird with nostrils at the end of its bill.

FEBRUARY 14

In 1929, members of Al Capone's gang killed seven unarmed men, because they were part of 'Bugs' Moran's rival gang. The event became known as the St Valentine's Day Massacre. The killers surprised their victims by dressing up as policemen.

The German Army issues hairnets to servicemen who want to wear their hair long.

A sloth can move twice as fast through water as it can on dry land.

Spain literally means 'the land of rabbits'.

Atilla the Hun is thought to have been a dwarf.

FEBRUARY (15)

Galileo, who was born in 1564, broke with convention by openly living with his mistress, Marina Gamba, for ten years. Of the three children they produced, the son became a lawyer, and the two daughters both became nuns.

A snail can have about twenty-five thousand teeth.

Three-quarters of the chemical energy of petrol is wasted when it is used in a motor-car.

The moon is four hundred times smaller than the sun, but it is also four hundred times nearer to the earth. That is why there can be a perfect eclipse.

A large-sized whale needs at least three tons of food a day.

FEBRUARY (16)

Francis Galton, who was born on 16 February 1822, was one of the major proposers of a new science called 'eugenics'. Among his ideas were the enforced sterilization of sub-standard people, and the systematic creation of a more superior race of human beings. His views found a platform in various eminent journals, and were supported by such luminaries as H.G. Wells and George Bernard Shaw.

Giraffes are not able to cough.

We eat an average of one hundred and forty thousand pounds of food in our lifetime.

Sir Isaac Newton, one of the most influential scientists of all time, was obsessed with the occult and the supernatural.

Many sailors used to wear gold earrings so that they could always afford a proper burial when they died.

FEBRUARY (17)

Geronimo, the great Apache leader, died today in 1908. Late in his life he joined the Dutch Reformed Church, but was thrown out for gambling. His real name was not Geronimo, but Goyathlay which literally means 'one who yawns'.

Spiders' webs are traditionally a natural clotting agent. If they are applied to a cut, they are meant to stop the flow of blood, and help it to heal quickly.

The erect penis of the rabbit flea is the most complicated to be found on any animal.

Squids can commit suicide by eating their own tentacles.

A Boeing 707 uses four thousand gallons of petrol to reach the top of its take-off climb.

FEBRUARY (18)

On this day in 1965, Gambia became independent. It is the smallest nation on the African Continent, and its official language is English.

By the time you have read this sentence, you will have been bombarded by air molecules more than one hundred billion billion times.

Whatever its size or thickness, no piece of paper can be folded in half more than seven times.

British women high-jumpers have missed out on the gold medal at every Olympics between 1936 and 1960. On each occasion they took the silver medal.

Idi Amin bought over one thousand kilts for his marching bands.

FEBRUARY 19

Charles Blondin, the greatest tightrope-walker of his age, and the first man to cross the Niagara Falls on a three-inch rope, died today in 1897. He once walked across the Falls with his agent on his back.

Each time you 'crack' a whip, the end of it has to travel at the speed of sound.

Approximately four million people attended the open-air funeral of President Nasser of Egypt.

According to numerous polls, the physical attribute women find most attractive in men is a small pair of buttocks.

The French eat about five hundred million snails a year.

FEBRUARY 20

Ralph and Carolyn Cummins had five children between 1952 and 1966. All five were born on the same day — today.

Some of the hotels in Las Vegas put gambling tables outside, and a few even go as far as having them floating in the swimming pool.

St John the Evangelist was the only one of the Twelve Apostles to die a natural death.

Per head, the Swiss are the world's biggest consumers of cheese.

In the sixteenth century, it was thought improper to wear a nightdress in bed.

FEBRUARY (21)

On this day in 1907, the famous English poet W.H. Auden was born. He was a homosexual, but in 1936 he agreed to marry Erika Mann so that she could obtain a British passport. They met for the first time on their wedding day.

Sir Winston Churchill rationed himself to fifteen cigars a day.

Only male canaries are able to sing.

A ten-gallon hat in fact only holds about three-quarters of a gallon.

During the chariot scene in 'Ben Hur', a small red car can be seen driving by in the distance.

FEBRUARY (22)

Edward Kennedy, who stood for the Democratic nomination in 1980 and is a member of the famous Kennedy family, was born today in 1932. While he was at Harvard College, he was suspended for cheating in a Spanish exam.

When you blush, your stomach-lining also becomes redder.

The children's nursery rhyme, 'Ring-A-Ring-A-Roses', actually refers to the Black Death, which killed around thirty million people in the fourteenth century.

The actress, Tuesday Weld, was born on a Friday.

When Krakatoa erupted in 1883, the sound was heard in Texas, USA.

FEBRUARY (23)

Samuel Pepys, the English writer, was born today in 1633. According to his famous diary, his wife often complained of his continuous squeezing of their maid's breasts in the mornings. Pepys also admits to a voracious capacity for reading seventeenth-century pornographic books.

At their nearest point, Russia and America are only two miles apart.

The Yo-Yo originated in The Philippines, where it was used as a weapon in hunting.

Mexico once had three different Presidents in the space of just one day.

Hindus do not like dying in bed. They prefer to come to rest beside a river.

FEBRUARY (24)

On 24 February 1500, Charles V, one of the greatest in an illustrious line of holy Roman Emperors, was born. He was a man of many talents, and was a particularly gifted linguist. He is credited with the following statement: 'I speak Spanish to God, Italian to women, French to men, and German to my horse'.

There are more kinds of insects in the world than **all** kinds of other animals put together.

Many centuries ago, orange rinds were used as contraceptive diaphragms.

Every time a fly lands on an ocean liner, it causes it to sink lower in the water by a microscopic amount — but it causes it to sink nevertheless.

If our ears were only slightly more sensitive, we would experience the constant background noise of molecules colliding in the air.

FEBRUARY 25

The great opera singer, Enrico Caruso, was born on this day in 1873. He made over £3 million during his career, and one of his favourite places to practise was in the bath. He often bathed twice a day, and had a special music rack fitted by the bath itself, while a pianist accompanied him from a nearby room.

There is only one bird which can fly backwards — the humming-bird.

The word 'denim' entered the language because the fabric originally came from the French city of Nimes. It was consequently labelled 'de Nimes'.

It is thought that some unborn babies dream.

FEBRUARY 26

The French writer, Victor Hugo, was born today in 1802. He had a habit of asking his servant to steal his clothes in the morning. This meant he could not go outside, and so was forced to carry on writing.

Polar bears can reach speeds of up to twenty-five miles an hour.

In the north of Norway, the sun shines day and night for three-and-a-half months each summer.

The national flag of Italy was designed by Napoléon Bonaparte.

The human nervous system can relay messages to and from the brain at speeds of up to two hundred miles an hour.

FEBRUARY (27)

The English actress, Elizabeth Taylor, was born in London on this day in 1929. The highly expensive film 'Cleopatra', in which she took the leading role, was banned in Egypt in 1963 because she was a Jewish convert.

When George I became King of England in 1714, his wife did not join him as Queen. Instead, accusing her of being an adultress, he had her put under house arrest for thirty-two years.

An estimated 1,500 million people watched the final of the 1982 World Cup.

Baden-Powell's Scout Movement had a membership of over one hundred and fifty thousand by the end of its first five years.

The population of the world could fit on to the Isle of Wight, though there would be standing-room only.

FEBRUARY (28)

The expatriate American novelist, Henry James, died on this day in 1916. An extensive traveller, he suffered from constipation for much of his life. Because of the constant pain and inconvenience, James himself said that it was like having terminal cancer.

The country Brazil got its name from its native Brazil-nut tree, and not the other way round.

Bees have five eyes.

Charles the Bald was the grandfather of Charles the Simple. Both were rulers of France.

FEBRUARY (29)

Up until the 1930s, 29 February was the feast of St Oswald of Worcester. Then someone decided that St Oswald was missing out, having a feast-day only once every four years, and it was moved to 28 February.

Lord Byron kept a trained bear in his room while he was at Cambridge.

The hippopotamus is born under water.

About one-quarter of the world's population lives in China.

Illegal gambling dens in eighteenth-century England employed a man who had only one job — to swallow the evidence if the place was raided.

MARCH

Pauline Masters, the shortest person of all time, died in 1895, her death largely caused by an excess of alcohol.

I was born on 14 March 1933 (a couple of months after the National Playing Fields Association had been given its Royal Charter). Albert Einstein was celebrating his fifty-fourth birthday (he'd been born only six weeks after the action at Rorkes Drift). Meanwhile, the body-line bowling controversy was raging in Australia and 'The Kid From Spain', starring Eddie Cantor, was about to open in the West End. A year earlier to the day, George Eastman, the great pioneer of photography, had gone to meet his Maker.

MARCH ① 1

Pauline Masters, widely held to be the shortest person of all time, died today in 1895, at the age of nineteen. Her twelve brothers and sisters were all of normal stature, but Pauline never grew to a height of more than twenty-three inches. Her premature death was largely caused by an excess of alcohol.

Whales increase in weight thirty thousand million times in their first two years.

All the planets in our Solar System could fit inside a hollow Jupiter.

John Wilkes Booth, the man who assassinated President Lincoln, was not unknown before he fired the fateful shot. In fact, he was a famous matinée idol who received many fan letters every day.

The human nervous system can relay messages to and from the brain at speeds of up to two hundred miles an hour.

MARCH ② 2

On this day in 1972, the spaceship, Pioneer 10, took off into the air at an amazing speed. Its mission was to go further than any previous spaceship, and break out of our own Solar System. It reached the moon in under half a day, and is expected to continue travelling for another two million years.

While they consider defecating to be socially acceptable, the Australian Aborigines will not allow themselves to be seen eating in public.

Having survived trench warfare during the First World War, a South African monkey was awarded a medal and promoted to the rank of corporal.

People in Tibet stick their tongues out at each other as a sign of respect.

You often carry cold viruses in the palms of your hands.

MARCH (3)

Alexander Graham Bell, the inventor of the telephone, was born on 3 March 1824. Though he was responsible for the invention of one of the most important communication systems of the modern era, neither his mother nor his wife would have been able to reap the benefits, because both (ironically) were deaf.

Not only is a python able to eat a pig whole, but it is also able to fast for over a year at a time.

The Burmese are fond of watching fish fight, and sometimes gamble on the outcome.

Only one-twentieth of all children are born on the day predicted by doctors.

Dorothy Pentreath is said to have been the last person to speak Ancient Cornish as her mother tongue. She died in 1777.

MARCH (4)

Marlon Brando was born on this day in 1924. During a stormy career, he has won two Oscars as an actor in a leading role — for 'On The Waterfront' and 'The Godfather'. He has what might be called a love-hate relationship with the film industry, and was once quoted as saying: 'An actor's a guy who, if you ain't talking about him, ain't listening.'

Crocodiles carry their young in their mouths.

The infamous Roman Emperor Nero was an orphan.

The nerve fibres in the body of the giant squid are five hundred times thicker than our own.

MARCH 5

The Russian leader, Stalin, died on 5 March 1953. By all accounts, he had a rather odd physical appearance, with one arm longer than the other and a face scarred by a dose of smallpox.

Over £20,000-worth of blank ammunition is used each year in Britain for purely ceremonial purposes.

The largest carnivorous mammal in the world is the Alaskan brown bear.

The French equivalent of 'The quick brown fox jumped over the lazy dog', a sentence which uses all the letters of the alphabet and is useful when learning to type, is '**Allez porter ce vieux whisky au juge blond qui fume un Havane**.' Roughly translated, this means: 'Go and take this old whisky to the fair-haired judge smoking the Havana cigar.'

Sloths spend over 75% of their lives asleep.

MARCH 6

The Victorian poet, Elizabeth Barrett Browning, was born today in 1806. She was bedridden for most of her life, as the result of a spinal injury at the age of fifteen. Her love affair with the poet, Robert Browning, has become a romantic legend, and it is said that she died in his arms.

Man is the only animal capable of smiling.

There are more people in Monaco's State Symphony Orchestra than there are in its Army.

A giraffe's neck contains the same number of vertebrae as a human's.

An average of over ten people a year are killed by lightning in Britain alone.

MARCH (7)

Maurice Ravel, the French composer who was born today in 1875, entered the prestigious Paris Conservatoire at the age of only fourteen. Though he was always a frail person, he insisted on enlisting as a truck driver at the Front during World War One, but soon had to be discharged as the strain was too much.

Every day, over 45,000 people attend the theatre and concert halls in Moscow.

In 1911, three men were hanged for the murder of Sir Edmund Berry at Greenbury Hill — they were called Green, Berry, and Hill.

Twenty thousand people attended the public cremation of Dr William Price, who was a leading nineteenth-century campaigner for the right of people to be cremated.

MARCH (8)

King William III of England died on 8 March 1702. His death was the direct result of being thrown from his horse a few days earlier, after it had unsuspectingly tripped over a molehill.

If you were lucky enough to live in California, you could enter your pet frog in one of their many public frog-jumping competitions.

Siamese Buddhists leave a tuft of hair on their otherwise bald heads so that Buddha has something to grab when he eventually lifts them up to Heaven.

Whale sharks can be as much as sixty feet long. Apparently, they wouldn't dream of trying to attack any large animal, such as man.

The first pancakes and the first pancake races came about as a result of using up stocks of food that were banned during Lent.

MARCH (9)

Ernest Bevin, the Minister of Labour in Britain during the Second World War, was born today in 1881. He was one of the most influential politicians of his age, and is considered the architect of the Welfare State. His education, however, was short — he left school at the tender age of eleven.

During the 1920s, the Royal Opera House in London served as a public dance-hall.

It is illegal to be a prostitute in Siena, Italy, if your name is Mary.

Many male fishes blow bubbles when they want to copulate with a female.

About seventy per cent of the living organisms in the world are bacteria.

MARCH (10)

Attacks on public works of art are not a wholly new phenomenon. Back in 1914, on 10 March, a group of Suffragettes walked into the National Gallery in London, and attacked Velasquez's painting known as the 'Rokeby Venus', in order to draw attention to their cause.

In Ancient Peru, when a woman found an ugly potato in the ground, it was the custom for her to push it into the face of the nearest man.

Much more money is spent on cigarettes and alcohol in Britain, than on life insurance.

Henry III of France used to hang a basket full of small dogs around his neck.

The Russian composer, Borodin, was really only an amateur musician. His full-time occupation was as a Professor of Chemistry.

MARCH (11)

Harold Wilson, former Labour Prime Minister of Britain, was born on 11 March 1916. Asked once what was required to become a successful politician, Mr Wilson replied: 'The greatest asset a head of state can have is the ability to get a good night's sleep.'

Aircraft Recognition, by R.A. Saville-Smith, published in 1941, has sold over seven million copies.

There is a worm which lives under the eyelid of the hippopotamus, and feeds off the animal's 'tears'.

Transporting the corpses off the battlefield for proper burial was a major problem for the medieval Crusaders. They solved their problem by taking with them to the Holy Wars huge cauldrons for boiling the bodies. Bones were much lighter and easier to carry.

Nero's wife had five hundred asses at her disposal to keep her bath continually topped up with fresh milk.

MARCH (12)

The Russian ballet dancer and choreographer, Nijinsky, was born today in 1890. He shared many great triumphs with his one-time lover, the impresario Diaghilev, but in 1917, at the age of twenty-seven, he had a mental breakdown and never worked again.

President Kaunda of Zambia once threatened to resign if his fellow countrymen didn't stop drinking so much alcohol. The President himself was teetotal.

Over half the men in Corfu are called Spiro.

The only wild camels in the world are to be found in Australia.

Some moral purists in the Middle Ages believed that women's ears ought to be covered up because the Virgin Mary had conceived a child through them.

MARCH (13)

The planet Uranus has only been known for two hundred years. It was discovered by Sir William Herschel on 13 March 1781.

The lance ceased to be an official battle weapon in the British Army in 1927.

Every day, the streets and parks of London are doused with over one hundred thousand gallons of urine.

There is a tribe in Africa whose women members have a rather gruesome way of making themselves more attractive. They deliberately cut their own faces to leave permanent raised scars.

When tea first arrived in America, many people consumed the leaves and not the water in which they had been boiled.

MARCH (14)

One of the most creative intellects of all time, Albert Einstein, was born on 14 March 1879. Unfortunately, his final words are lost to posterity. The nurse who was looking after him when he died did not understand German.

Europeans who first came across the giraffe called the animal a 'camelopard', thinking it a cross between a camel and a leopard.

The rare metal, gallium, will melt if you hold it in your hand for any length of time.

The smallest trees in the world are the dwarf willows of Greenland. They are about two inches tall.

A mosquito has forty-seven teeth.

MARCH 15

Julius Caesar was murdered on this day in 44 BC. It is said that the reason he always wore a laurel wreath was because he didn't want anyone to know that he was going bald.

In the late nineteenth century, it became fashionable for women to have their nipples pierced in order to sport a gold or jewelled ring.

Since the turn of the century, every elected President of America has been taller than his rival for the White House.

More fish and chips are sold at Labour Party conferences than at those held by the Conservatives.

If food is very short, the ribbon worm can eat up to ninety-five per cent of its own body, and still survive.

MARCH 16

Aubrey Beardsley was one of the most influential artists and illustrators of the last century. However, his career only lasted six years, and he died on 16 March 1898 at the tender age of twenty-five.

During the seventeenth century, the Sultan of Turkey ordered the drowning of his entire harem of women. He then promptly created a new one.

Hindu men believe it is unlucky to marry for a third time. If a man does wish to take a third wife, he can avoid misfortune by marrying a tree first. The tree (his third wife) is then burnt, and he is free to marry the woman of his choice.

The Amayra guides of Bolivia are said to be able to keep pace with a trotting horse for a distance of sixty miles.

MARCH (17)

The day, 17 March, belongs to the missionary priest, Patrick, who later became the patron saint of Ireland. Though his history is rather confused, and cannot be laid down with any certainty, there is one thing we can be sure of — St Patrick was not Irish.

A group of toads is called a 'knot'.

Fillings in people's teeth have been known to pick up radio waves.

So far this century, the weight of the leaning tower of Pisa has decreased by about three hundred tons.

Queen Victoria never spoke English perfectly. Her mother tongue was German.

MARCH (18)

Ivan the Terrible died on 18 March 1584. He was a ruthless tyrant, who thought nothing of mass murder and vicious torture. He once claimed to have deflowered over one thousand virgins and to have butchered a similar number of their resulting offspring.

The underwater explorer, Jacques Cousteau, invented the aqualung while serving with the French Resistance during World War Two.

It was only at the last minute that Amundsen decided to set off for the South Pole. His original plan was for another exploration of its northern equivalent. He is now remembered as the first man to reach the bottommost tip of the world, beating the doomed party led by Captain Scott.

An electric eel produces an average of four hundred volts.

MARCH (19)

Sergei Diaghilev was born on this day in 1872. His original ambition was to be a classical composer, but he was advised against this by the famous Russian musician Rimsky-Korsakov. Diaghilev settled instead for the world of dancing, and has some claim to the title of 'The Father of Modern Ballet'.

Dr Johnson is said to have once drunk thirty-six glasses of port during the course of an evening.

It was quite common for the men of Ancient Greece to do their exercises in public, without a stitch of clothing on.

Within a pride of lions, ninety per cent of the hunting is done by the females.

Paper was invented early in the second century by a Chinese eunuch.

MARCH (20)

Sir Isaac Newton, one of the most important scientists who has ever lived, died on this day in 1727. His sex life was literally a non-starter, and it is thought that at the time of his death he was still a virgin.

The Amazon River has over a thousand tributary streams.

If the contents of the oceans were evenly distributed among us, every person on this earth would receive over one hundred billion gallons of water.

Engels, who helped Marx write **The Communist Manifesto**, owned a business in Manchester.

During the nineteenth century, tomato ketchup was sold as a medicine.

MARCH (21)

Johann Sebastian Bach was born on 21 March 1685. He came from an extraordinary musical family, with over fifty of his relatives pursuing a career in music.

Bamboo can grow over three feet in the space of twenty-four hours.

John Milton, who is famous for writing the epic poem 'Paradise Lost', spent much of his life writing revolutionary manifestos.

A cheetah can reach a speed of forty-five miles an hour from a standing start, in two seconds.

Admiral Lord Nelson was only five feet two inches tall.

MARCH (22)

J.B. Lully, the greatest French composer of his age, died in rather unusual circumstances on this day in 1687. He was conducting a concert when, in a moment of frenzy, he pierced his own foot with the pointed baton he liked to use. The resulting gangrene proved fatal.

Before Persia became Iran officially in 1935, it was called Iran.

Sir Winston Churchill had such a prodigious memory that he could recite an entire Shakespeare play verbatim.

Fewer than a quarter of the inhabitants of India can speak the country's official language of Hindi.

Halley's Comet will next be visible in 1986.

MARCH (23)

The French writer, Stendahl, died today in 1842. His love life was not a very happy one — he caught VD from his very first lover at the age of twenty-eight, and suffered the disease for the rest of his life.

The three largest circulation daily newspapers in the world are all Russian.

The Russian revolutionary, Leon Trotsky, once appeared in a Hollywood silent movie as an extra.

Fourteen million people died during World War One. Twenty million people died in a 'flu epidemic just afterwards.

Alaska is over twice the size of Texas.

MARCH (24)

The Grand National of 1956 was a race of great drama. Millions watched as the Queen Mother's horse Devon Loch, cleared the final fence in the lead, seeming certain to win. Suddenly, as the horse neared the finishing line, it collapsed, losing the race, and depriving the crowd of the first royal win this century. The unfortunate rider was none other than Dick Francis, later a best-selling writer.

Catherine the First of Russia made it a rule that no man was allowed to get drunk at her parties before nine o'clock.

Gold is the sixteenth most rare chemical element.

The Ancient Egyptians trained baboons to wait at their tables.

There are over two hundred different religious denominations in the US.

MARCH (25)

On 25 March 1964, the British Government set aside an acre of the famous turf at Runnymede, where the Magna Carta was signed, as a memorial to the late John F. Kennedy.

Every cubic mile of seawater contains an average of one hundred and fifty million tons of minerals.

In the middle of the nineteenth century, the circus impresario P.T. Barnum tried to buy the house where Shakespeare was born. He failed, and it is now a national monument.

Ever since the sixth century, the Imperial Throne of Japan has been occupied by just one family.

A functional flush toilet was found in the palace at Knossos. The city dates back to 2000 BC.

Napoleon had a pathological fear of cats.

MARCH (26)

The great French actress, Sarah Bernhardt, died on 26 March 1923. She had one of her legs amputated in 1915, but continued to act until her death, playing roles specifically created to suit her disability.

There were nearly two hundred armed revolts in Bolivia during the first hundred years of its independence from Spanish rule.

Though anything to do with the occult was considered heresy by the Roman Catholic Church, Pope Julius II set the time of his Coronation in 1503 according to the stars.

Men have an average of ten per cent more red blood cells than women.

The Sahara Desert is as large as America.

MARCH (27)

King James I of England died on 27 March 1625. After Sir Walter Raleigh had introduced tobacco to England, King James wrote what might be called the first Government health warning — a booklet condemning smoking as dangerous and anti-social.

Forty per cent of the inhabitants of Sweden have surnames ending in 'son'.

For thirteen years, the composer Tchaikovsky was financed by a wealthy widow. He never found out the identity of this mysterious benefactor, because the gift was conditional on one thing — that the two of them should never meet.

The speed of the earth's rotation at its fastest point (the equator) is about one thousand miles per hour.

There are over ten thousand golf courses in the US.

MARCH (28)

In the last hundred years, there have been four natural disasters on 28 March. In 1888, Wellington, New Zealand was struck by a devastating tidal wave; in 1920, a tornado hit Chicago, USA, causing over a million pounds' worth of damage; in 1965, an earthquake devastated Chile, and five years later another hit western Turkey, killing over one thousand people.

Eleanor of Aquitaine, who was married to Henry II of England, set up and presided over a unique set of Courts, called the Courts of Love. Abstract love problems were discussed, and solemn judgements were made.

Gorillas often sleep for up to fourteen hours a day.

Even the most advanced telescope would find it difficult to see anything less than half a mile across on the surface of the moon.

MARCH (29)

On 29 March 1461, the warring baronial houses of York and Lancaster clashed in a truly bloodthirsty battle. It was the largest confrontation of the famous Wars of the Roses, and by the end of the day the fields of Towton were littered with corpses. In a single day, two-thirds of the nobility of England lost their lives.

The male Californian sea-otter grips the nose of the female with his teeth during mating.

Princess Anne was the only competitor at the 1976 Montreal Olympics who did not have to undergo a sex test.

An approaching car has a shriller noise than one going away.

There are no clocks in the casinos at Las Vegas.

MARCH (30)

On 30 March 1867, Alaska was officially purchased by the United States. At the time many American politicians criticized the move, believing such a wasteland to be a costly folly. Over the years, however, Alaska has proved to be an extremely profitable investment, reaping a large harvest of both oil and gold.

Over half the people in Great Britain enter the Football Pools every week.

Lions are exported to Africa by Windsor Safari Park in England.

At the height of German inflation in the 1920s, one US dollar was worth 4,000,000,000,000,000,000 marks.

La Paz in Bolivia is so high above sea level that the air has barely enough oxygen to support a fire.

MARCH (31)

Robert Bunsen, the man who gave his name to the laboratory burner which he helped to popularize, was born today in 1811. Ironically for someone who has contributed to the increased safety of chemical laboratories, he was somewhat accident-prone himself. On two occasions he survived fatal doses of arsenic, and in 1843 he lost his right eye in a laboratory explosion.

The average porcupine has over 30,000 quills.

When he was young and impoverished, Pablo Picasso kept warm by burning his own paintings.

Using radar, scientists have discovered mountains and lakes buried beneath the ice of the Antarctic.

The youngest Nobel prize-winner ever was called William Bragg. He shared the physics prize with his father when he was only twenty-three.

APRIL

An oyster can change its sex from male to female and back again many times during its lifetime.

This is Shakespeare's month, marking both his birth and death. He and I only once had dealings – in the television version of Hamlet (the one with Christopher Plummer in the lead), and in which I played Horatio. The play was shot on location in Elsinore Castle, Shakespeare's own setting, though none of us had reckoned on the foghorn, built in the intervening three hundred and sixty years, that boomed out every fifteen minutes. We'd planned to shoot in long scenes, but ended up snatching short takes between one blast and the next. Happily, the finished version didn't give this away.

APRIL 1

On this day in 1954, Mrs P. Ride, a mother of five, took out the historic patent on sliced bread. It is widely considered one of the most important inventions of the twentieth century, and though many people have claimed to match it, few have succeeded.

An oyster can change its sex from male to female and back again many times during its lifetime.

It took two weeks for Europe to learn of President Lincoln's death, proving that even the most important news doesn't always travel fast.

The second most common atom to hydrogen is not oxygen as you might expect, but helium.

Turkeys often look up at the sky during a rainstorm. Unfortunately many drown as a result.

APRIL 2

Charlemagne, the first Holy Roman Emperor, was born today in about 742. Some chroniclers of the time describe him as a giant, for in an age when the average height was well below that of today, he is said to have been over seven feet tall.

Even the smallest volcano has more potential power at its disposal than the largest earthquake or hurricane.

Ninety-nine per cent of all the forms of life that have ever existed on the earth are now extinct.

There is a multi-storey brothel in Hamburg, Germany, which operates with the tacit approval of the Government.

During the Middle Ages, the Clergy, almost without exception, were the only people who were able to read and write.

APRIL (3)

Washington Irvine, the American writer and historian, was born on this day in 1783. He got the idea for the character Rip Van Winkle from the legend of the Cretan poet, Epimenides, who decided to take a short nap while out hunting, and didn't wake up for fifty years.

John D. Rockefeller gave away over five hundred million dollars during his lifetime.

It is harder to reach the speed of sound at sea-level than it is high up in the air.

The German writer, Thomas Mann, took a break of thirty-two years between the start and finish of his novel, **The Confessions of Felix Krull**.

In California, it is illegal to kill or threaten a butterfly.

APRIL (4)

The American Civil Rights leader, Martin Luther King, was assassinated on 4 April 1968. Back in 1941, when he was only twelve years old, Dr King became so depressed that he twice attempted suicide by jumping out of his bedroom window.

Lightning is essential to the survival of plant life on this planet, because the intense heat it generates when it hits our air supply transforms nitrogen into the nitrates which plants feed off.

It was considered highly unfashionable for Venetian women during the Renaissance to have anything but silvery-blonde hair.

Three million Russians have died in the Siberian labour camps.

The Tower of London has served many purposes in its time, and once even housed a zoo.

APRIL 5

On 5 April 1955, Sir Winston Churchill resigned as Prime Minister of Great Britain. And on exactly the same day twenty-one years later, Prime Minister Harold Wilson also announced his decision to step down.

The writer, Somerset Maugham, worked for British Intelligence during World War One.

The southernmost tip of Africa is not the Cape of Good Hope as most people think, but Cape Agulhas.

Hedgehogs couldn't survive without fleas, because fleas provide essential stimulation to their skin.

Urine was once used to wash clothes.

APRIL 6

The late Sir John Betjeman, who became Britain's Poet Laureate, was born on this day in 1906. His poetry was largely concerned with the disappearing traditions of country and provincial life, and it was always unpretentious. When he was asked just after the Second World War what he would have liked to do other than write poetry, he replied that he would like 'to be a stationmaster on a small country branch-line (single track)'.

Because their eyeballs are fixed, whales have to move their whole body in order to shift their line of vision.

In the two years after the first 'talkie' appeared, American cinemas attracted over one hundred million people a week.

At the centre of the sun, the temperature can be as high as twenty million degrees centigrade.

APRIL (7)

According to a tradition dating back to the sixth century, the first cuckoo of the year appears on 7 April at a town called St Brynach in Wales.

The Palace of Versailles in France has over a thousand fountains scattered around its grounds.

A single ounce of gold can be beaten into a thin film covering a hundred square feet.

Blackbird, who was the chief of the Omaha Indians, was buried sitting on his favourite horse.

'Mummies' are so-called because of the wax (or 'mum') which is smeared on to the bandages for waterproofing.

APRIL (8)

A great earthquake had been predicted for London on this day in 1750, and in order to avoid the full force of it, many people decided to spend the previous night in Hyde Park. The earthquake, however, never materialized.

The city of Damascus has been continuously inhabited since 2000 BC

The heart of the giraffe is two feet long, and can weigh as much as twenty-four pounds.

The aquatic animal, the Red Sponge, can be broken into a thousand pieces and still reconstitute itself.

Marie Curie, who twice won the Nobel Prize, and discovered radium, was not allowed to become a member of the prestigious French Academy because she was a woman.

APRIL (9)

The actress, Mrs Patrick Campbell, died on 9 April 1940. She was one of Hollywood's wits and once said of the vampish Tallulah Bankhead: 'Tallulah is always skating on thin ice. Everyone wants to be around when it breaks.'

Lenin's real name was Vladimir Ilyich Ulyanov, but Lenin was not his only pseudonym. He used one hundred and fifty others during his life.

The original name for the United Nations was the 'Associated Powers'.

For the Athenians of the Golden Age, homosexuality was the highest form of love, since only men could operate as equals.

Over two hundred different languages are spoken throughout the Soviet Union.

APRIL

On 10 April 1932, Paul Von Hindenburg was re-elected as President of Germany. He got nineteen million votes. Hitler got thirteen million.

Between 1920 and 1932, the Finnish runner, Paavo Nurmi, won nine Olympic gold medals.

Though it is forbidden by the Government, many Indians still adhere to the caste system which says that it is a defilement for even the shadow of a person from a lowly caste to fall on a Brahman (a member of the highest priestly caste).

Only one American President has been a bachelor — James Buchanan.

During World War One the future Pope John XXIII was a sergeant in the Italian Army.

APRIL (11)

John Merrick, the 'Elephant Man', died on this day in 1890. He got his name because he was deformed by elephantiasis, a disease which causes some parts of the body to blow up out of all proportion. His head was so large that he had to sleep with it resting on his knees, and it was probably the weight of it which dislocated his neck and caused his death.

There are more Jews in America than in the whole of the State of Israel.

December 25 was not celebrated as the birthday of Jesus Christ until AD 440.

There are more miles of canals in Birmingham than there are in Venice.

Madame Tallien, a member of Louis XIV's Court, used to bathe in crushed strawberries whenever they were available.

APRIL (12)

Upon the death of F.D. Roosevelt, Harry S. Truman became President of America on this day in 1945. The initial 'S' in the middle of his name doesn't, in fact, mean anything. Both his grandfathers had names beginning with 'S', and so Truman's mother didn't want to disappoint either of them.

A lunar day is two minutes and five seconds an hour less than a normal day.

In the late nineteenth century, some people were able to vote as many as three times — once at their homes, once at their offices in the City of London, and once at their universities.

Between the two World Wars, France was controlled by forty different governments.

The Pacific Ocean fills nearly half the globe.

APRIL (13)

The first public performance of Handel's 'Messiah' took place on 13 April 1742. It was a great achievement not only because of the quality of the music, but because Handel had suffered a stroke five years earlier at the age of fifty-two.

There are over five thousand islands in the group called The Philippines.

New York City passed a law in 1978 which requires dog owners to clean up after their pets or face a fine.

In eighteenth-century Portugal, the Church owned two-thirds of all the land.

The water in the Dead Sea is so salty that it is far easier to float than to drown.

APRIL (14)

President Abraham Lincoln was assassinated on 14 April 1865 by the actor John Wilkes Booth. Booth was so nervous before the event that he consumed at least one bottle of spirits during the hours leading up to the shooting at 10.15 pm. His accomplice, who was meant to shoot Vice-President Andrew Johnson, became too drunk to fire.

William Shakespeare was not only a writer; he was also a professional actor.

St Teresia Benedicta à Cruce is the only Roman Catholic Saint of modern times who was a Jew.

Louis Braille, who invented the Braille system of reading for the blind, was himself blind from the age of three.

A germ is not necessarily dirty or harmful — it is the name given to any small scrap of life.

APRIL (15)

On 15 April 1912 the SS **Titanic** sunk on her maiden voyage and over 1,500 people died. Fourteen years earlier a novel was published by Morgan Robertson which seemed to foretell the disaster. The book described a ship the same size as the **Titanic** which crashes into an iceberg on its maiden voyage on a misty April night. The name of Robertson's fictional ship was the **Titan**.

Most plant pollen will ignite and cause a small explosion if it falls on a very hot surface.

Frank Sinatra was once quoted as saying that rock 'n' roll was only played by 'cretinous goons'.

The diameter of the sphere of the observable universe is twenty-five billion light years.

APRIL (16)

Madame Tussaud, whose waxworks are one of the most popular tourist attractions in London, died today in 1850. During the French Revolution her model-making skills were employed in making death masks for the victims of the dreaded guillotine.

Holland is the most densely populated country in the world, with over a thousand people per square mile.

Americans spend four times as much per year on pet food as they do on baby food.

For the first six years of his life the German poet, Rilke, was treated as if he were a girl. His mother dressed him up in skirts, and called him Sophie.

In 1738 the Spanish made the mistake of cutting off the ear of a British naval captain, beginning the aptly named 'War of Jenkins' Ear'.

APRIL 17

The Budget speech of this day in 1956 saw the introduction of Premium Savings Bonds into Britain. The machine which picks the winning numbers is called 'Ernie', an acronym standing for 'electronic random number indicator equipment'.

After it has bitten someone and is bloated with blood, a mosquito can carry twice its own weight and still fly.

As a response to the Great Plague, the so-called Flagellants of Germany used to beat themselves and each other in an attempt to appease God's wrath.

Lloyd's of London, who boast that they will insure anything, do not do life insurance.

The symptoms of haemophilia are never displayed by women, but only they can pass it on. With men it is the opposite way round.

APRIL 18

On this day in 1775, Paul Revere made his famous ride from Charleston to Lexington to warn the Colonists of the approach of the British Army. When he was younger, Paul Revere was a dentist.

For reasons of security, only people who were illiterate were considered for more routine jobs at the first atomic bomb construction centre in New Mexico.

Following Aristotle, the scientists of the Middle Ages believed that the heart — and not the brain — was the seat of human intelligence.

Honey is used to fill the centres of golf balls.

Since records started being kept, over sixty million harp seals have been killed in Newfoundland alone.

APRIL 19

Charles Darwin, the English naturalist who formed the theory of evolution, died on this day in 1882. Like Churchill, he did very poorly at school, and it was only his passion for natural history which secured him a berth on HMS **Beagle**. The voyage became a history-making one, with Darwin using his findings from the trip to develop his famous theory.

One in eight people in the world today suffers from chronic malnutrition.

Opium was used widely as a painkiller during the American Civil War. As a result, over one hundred thousand soldiers had become drug addicts by the end of the war.

Half the world lives in just four countries — China, Russia, America and India. The other half is spread over the remaining one hundred and sixty or so.

APRIL 20

The prostitutes sent to Emperor Louis Napoleon, who was born today in 1808, were instructed never to touch his Imperial face during intercourse. They were procured by his wife who supervised the extensive and meticulous washing they received before getting down to business.

The name given to the atomic bomb is rather misleading, because almost any explosion involves an atomic reaction. The atomic bomb involves a **nuclear** reaction.

According to the psychic fraternity, there is a higher density of ghosts in Britain than in any other country.

In Papua New Guinea there are villages within five miles of each other which speak different languages.

APRIL (21)

The American writer, Mark Twain, literally came and went with a bang. He was born on 30 November 1835 and died on this day in 1910. The famous Halley's Comet has appeared twice since the eighteenth century — first in 1835 and again in 1910.

Lightning is more likely than not to strike the same place twice, because it follows the path of least resistance.

There are more cars in Los Angeles than people.

Michael Faraday, the English scientist who discovered the principles of electromagnetic induction, refused a knighthood, preferring to remain plain Michael Faraday for the remainder of his life.

Every year the Isles of Scilly send sixty million blooms (mostly daffodils) to be sold in London's New Covent Garden flower market.

APRIL (22)

The Russian writer, Vladimir Nabokov, who was born today in 1899, wrote the controversial novel **Lolita**, which dealt with an older man's obsession with a teenage girl. Apart from being a contentious literary figure, Nabokov was obsessed with the more sedate hobby of butterfly-collecting.

A disease called progeria compresses your life cycle into just a few years. You will age around eight, and die when only twelve years old.

Male cats have barbs on their genitals, which cause the females to cry out in pain on withdrawal.

Sentenced to death by King Henry VIII, Anne Boleyn chose decapitation in preference to the more usual punishment for her crime of being burnt at the stake.

'The Society of Jesus' have never officially been called Jesuits, though it is the popular name for them.

APRIL (23)

By a strange coincidence, two of the greatest writers who have ever lived, William Shakespeare and Miguel de Cervantes (who wrote **Don Quixote**), both died on 23 April 1616.

In 1647 the English Parliament abolished Christmas.

Before it was stopped by the British, it was the custom for Indian women to be burnt alive on their husband's funeral pyre.

In the early twentieth century, rattlesnake venom was used to treat epilepsy.

If a surgeon in Ancient Egypt lost a patient while performing an operation, his hands were cut off.

APRIL (24)

The English novelist, Anthony Trollope, was born today in 1815. He wrote a phenomenal amount during his lifetime, completing fifty novels, and regularly composing a thousand words before breakfast. He also invented the pillar-box.

There are large colonies of scorpions living both in Kent and on the Central Line station of Ongar in Essex. Fortunately the variety is completely harmless.

During the nineteenth century, it was possible to travel from Scotland to Jerusalem by the old Roman roads, pausing only to make the two necessary sea-crossings.

The human heart beats faster during a heated argument than it does during sexual intercourse.

Some micro-organisms can only live where there is no oxygen.

APRIL (25)

King Edward II was born on this day in 1284. His death was a most unusual one — he was killed by a homosexual lover who shoved a red-hot poker into his anus.

We have muscles in our necks which, though now redundant and unworkable, were once meant to move our ears.

In 1870 twice as many books on religion were published as novels.

For three years the explorer Marco Polo was mayor of a city in China.

Molluscs are second only to insects as the most numerous living creatures on earth.

APRIL (26)

Although it is not known exactly when William Shakespeare was born, he was baptized on 26 April 1564. The works of this world-famous writer have been attributed to more than twenty other people, including Sir Walter Raleigh and Queen Elizabeth I. None of these claims has been proved.

In the seventeenth century nearly sixty million people are thought to have died in Europe from smallpox.

An atom is about a million times thinner than a human hair.

Because of its relatively small size, a humming-bird must eat constantly or risk death by starvation in a matter of hours.

If the entire history of the earth so far were to be compresssed into one calendar year, then mankind made its first appearance less than an hour ago.

APRIL (27)

On 27 April 1950, the State of Israel was officially recognized by the British Government. Ironically, the man who was perhaps the most crucial factor in the setting-up of Israel was the notorious anti-semite Stalin.

During the 1970s, Thomas Hardy was the most popular English language author in Japan.

Sir Isaac Newton was only twenty-three years old when he discovered the law of universal gravitation.

In Ancient Europe, people used olive oil to wash themselves.

If the covering membrane was removed, you could cut into you own brain and feel no pain.

APRIL (28)

The famous mutiny on the **Bounty**, led by Fletcher Christian against the evil Captain Bligh, began on this day in 1789. The subsequent fortunes of the two main protagonists were fairly mixed: Fletcher Christian's idyll on the South Seas island he made his home came to an end when he died four years later, while Bligh went on to become a Vice-Admiral, and later Governor of New South Wales.

There are over one hundred distinct ethnic groups living in the Soviet Union.

Coffee is the second largest item of international commerce in the world. The largest is petrol.

Peter the Great had the head of his wife's lover cut off and put into a jar of preserving alcohol, which he then ordered to be placed by her bed.

Cyanide is present in apple pips, but only in small doses.

APRIL 29

Sir Thomas Beecham, the English composer and conductor, was born on 29 April 1879. He was a man renowned for his learning and biting wit, and was once quoted as saying: 'Why do we have all these third-rate foreign conductors around — when we have so many second-rate ones of our own?'

To bury someone alive was considered an acceptable form of punishment in Mongolia.

There was a fall of black snow in Sweden in 1969.

The Great Wall of China took 1,700 years to build.

Every square-inch of human skin contains 625 sweat glands.

APRIL 30

Adolf Hitler committed suicide in a Berlin bunker on 30 April 1945. During his time in power in Germany, it was illegal for a policeman to call his dog Adolf.

A koala bear can survive by eating **only** the leaves of the eucalyptus tree.

Influenza got its name because people believed the illness was caused by the evil influence of the stars.

The two men who started the California Gold Rush — Sutter and Marshall — did not find any sizeable amounts of gold themselves, and both died poor men.

Cleopatra was not Egyptian but Macedonian.

MAY

French chemist, Louis Pasteur, was obsessive about his own hygiene and often refused to shake hands with anyone.

John Wayne was born on 26 May 1907. He taught me one valuable lesson that I have never forgotten. 'If you want to stay a star,' he said, 'talk low, talk slow and don't say too damned much.'

MAY (1)

The Scottish explorer, Dr David Livingstone, died on 1 May 1873. His body was brought back to England and buried in Westminster Abbey, but his heart literally remained in Africa, where he had spent so much of his life, because it was cut out and buried under a tree.

If your mouth was completely dry, you would not be able to distinguish the taste of anything.

The French chemist, Louis Pasteur, who pioneered the idea of pasteurization, was obsessive about his own hygiene, and often refused to shake hands with anyone.

Water freezes faster if cooled quickly from a warm temperature, than it does from a colder one.

Over three-quarters of a potato is water.

MAY (2)

Theodor Herzl, the Zionist leader who was born on this day in 1860, once had the astonishing idea of converting Jews to Christianity as a way of combating anti-Semitism.

A full-loaded supertanker travelling at normal speed takes at least twenty minutes to stop.

In the English hospitals of the seventeenth century, children were entitled to two gallons of beer as part of their weekly diet.

Horses were originally small animals, and had to be specially bred for riding.

In 1979 snow fell on the Sahara Desert for the first time in living memory.

MAY (3)

Benito Mussolini, the Italian dictator, welcomed Adolf Hitler to Rome on this day in 1938 to mark the start of their military alliance. Mussolini was apparently something of a handful at his boarding school when young. He was eventually expelled for stabbing a fellow pupil in the buttocks.

The Matami tribe of West Africa play a version of football, the only difference being that they use a human skull instead of a more normal ball.

It is usual for larger animals to live longer than smaller ones. Man is, however, the longest-living mammal, outstripping larger counterparts such as the elephant and the gorilla.

The English historian and theologian, the Venerable Bede, was the first person to date our history from the birth of Christ.

MAY (4)

The world's tallest building, the Sears Tower in Chicago, was finally 'topped off' on 4 May 1974. It has the same number of storeys as its closest rival, The World Trade Center (110), but at 1,454 feet, it is 104 feet higher.

Iceland is the world's oldest functioning democracy.

The magic word 'Abracadabra' was originally intended for the specific purpose of curing hay fever.

Men outnumber women in prisons by over thirty to one.

Einstein did not win his Nobel Prize in 1921 for his famous theory of Relativity, but for his work on photo-electric effects.

MAY (5)

Napoléon Bonaparte died on 5 May 1821 on the island of St Helena. One hundred and fifty years later, in 1971, his penis appeared for auction at Christie's in London. It didn't find a buyer.

In the early seventeenth century, over a thousand European children were kidnapped and shipped to the USA to become slaves.

Some locusts only survive for two weeks as an adult, after fifteen years as a small grub.

The scene where the king is deposed in Shakespeare's **Richard II**, was never allowed to be performed during the reign of Elizabeth I.

There are tiny fields of magnetism around the human heart and brain.

MAY (6)

Sigmund Freud, one of the most influential thinkers of the twentieth century, was born today in 1856. His first — and some would say most important — work, **The Interpretation of Dreams**, took eight years to sell its first printing of six hundred copies, and made Freud only just over a hundred pounds.

Queen Christina of Sweden had the pleasure of being tutored by the French philosopher, René Descartes.

The heart of Archbishop Cranmer was found intact amongst the ashes after he was burnt at the stake.

Human skin weighs a total of about six pounds.

Adolf Hitler's cook was Jewish.

MAY 7

King Alfonso XIII of Spain was born on 7 May 1886, but had to wait until his sixteenth birthday to become the official king of Spain. He was so tone deaf that he had to employ an 'anthem man' to tell him when the Spanish anthem was being played, so that he could stand up in reverence.

If all the gold produced in the world in the last five centuries were to be melted down and compressed, it could be made into a cube measuring fifty feet each side.

The largest egg in the world is the ostrich egg — it takes about forty minutes to hard-boil completely.

The commonest letter in both French and English is the letter 'e'. In 1969, a Frenchman managed to write a full-length novel called **La Disparition** which did not contain a single 'e'.

MAY 8

Gustave Flaubert, the French novelist, died on 8 May 1880. Some twenty-five years earlier his most famous novel, **Madame Bovary**, was published. Unfortunately some people thought that the sexual and moral content of the book left a lot to be desired, and Flaubert was actually charged with producing pornography. He eventually got off the charge, but the book itself was censored.

There are over one million tubes in the human kidney.

President Abraham Lincoln died believing himself to be illegitimate — he was mistaken.

Women used to tie holly on to the ends of their beds to stop themselves from becoming witches.

Only one person walked beside Mozart's coffin as it made its way to the cemetery where he was buried in an unmarked pauper's grave.

MAY 9

J.M. Barrie, who wrote the great children's story, **Peter Pan**, was born on this day in 1860. Barrie always liked to support young talent, and in 1919 he helped publish **The Young Visiters** by Daisy Ashford, which went on to sell nearly half a million copies. Amazingly, its authoress was a child of only nine when it was written

The Turks consider it very unlucky to step on a piece of bread.

Eau de Cologne was originally marketed as a way of protecting yourself against the plague.

All Sikhs take the name of 'Singh', meaning 'Lion-hearted'.

The only Shakespearean play which does not contain at least one song is 'The Comedy of Errors'.

MAY 10

The American dancer, Fred Astaire, was born on 10 May 1899. He was thought so valuable by his studio that they insured his legs for $650,000.

After the slaves' revolt led by Spartacus was crushed in 71 BC, six thousand slaves were crucified along Rome's main highway — the Appian Way.

The largest cell in the human body is the female reproductive cell, the ovum. The smallest is the male sperm.

Underneath the great icy plains of the Antarctic can sometimes be found little pools of unfrozen water.

If you travel from east to west across the Soviet Union, you will cross seven time zones.

MAY (11)

Irving Berlin, who was born on 11 May 1888 and who composed three thousand songs in his lifetime, couldn't read music.

In Thailand, kite-flying is a major sport with teams of up to twenty people competing against each other.

Ten per cent of the salt mined in the world each year is used to de-ice the roads in America.

Astronauts in orbit around the earth can see the wakes produced by passing boats.

Most people have lost fifty per cent of their taste buds by the time they reach the age of sixty.

MAY (12)

Augustus II, the Elector of Saxony and King of Poland, was born on 12 May 1670. He seemed to have a prodigious sexual appetite, and fathered hundreds of illegitimate children during his lifetime.

The British did not release the body of Napoléon Bonaparte to the French until twenty days after his death.

The human body contains about sixty thousand miles of blood vessels.

Elizabeth I of Russia had a wardrobe of fifteen thousand dresses.

Cancer claims forty victims an hour in America.

MAY 13

Joe Louis, whose reign as heavyweight champion of the world was the longest in history, was born on 13 May 1914. Before he won the world title, he was on the losing side against the German fighter, Max Schmeling, a defeat which Adolf Hitler saw as proof of the superiority of the white German race. The Führer was soon proved wrong, however, when Louis won the return match with ease.

Because they had no proper rubbish disposal system, the streets of ancient Mesopotamia became literally knee-deep in rubbish.

King Ptolemy IV of Egypt had a passion for large rowing boats. The biggest one needed ten thousand oarsmen to propel it through the water.

Sir Winston Churchill's mother was descended from a Red Indian.

MAY 14

Israel, proclaimed an independent State on 14 May 1948, has the highest military spending per capita of any country in the world.

The Goliath frog of West Africa is nearly three feet long.

Pablo Picasso was abandoned by the midwife just after his birth because she thought he was stillborn. He was saved by an uncle.

The power of the first hydrogen bomb tested in 1952 was equal to the combined power of all the bombs dropped on Germany and Japan in World War Two — including the atomic ones.

Sir Christopher Wren, the architect responsible for St Paul's Cathedral, built fifty-two churches in London in the space of forty-one years. His only architectural training had come in a six-month stint in Paris.

MAY (15)

On 15 May 1948, the Australian touring team scored a world record total of runs in one day. In just under six hours they made 721 all out against Essex, at Southchurch Park, Southend.

The mad Emperor Caligula once decided to go to war with the Roman God of the sea, Poseidon, and ordered his soldiers to throw their spears into the water at random.

Fred Astaire's first screen-test notes read: 'Can't act. Can't sing. Can dance a little.'

Sigmund Freud's friends paid the Nazis £20,000 to allow him out of Germany just before the start of World War Two. He died eighteen months later.

Only one Western film has ever been directed by a woman.

MAY (16)

The first Academy Awards (or 'Oscars') were presented on 16 May 1929. The most successful person in the history of these awards is undoubtedly Walt Disney. Between 1931 and 1969 he collected thirty-five 'Oscars'.

The River Nile has frozen over only twice in living memory — once in the ninth century, and then again in the eleventh century.

St Francis of Assisi, who preached in favour of renunciation of all wealth, came from a very rich family.

On average an acre of green land contains some fifty thousand spiders.

During the eighteenth century, laws had to be brought in to curb the seemingly insatiable appetite for gin amongst the poor. Their annual intake was as much as five million gallons.

MAY (17)

The Siege of Mafeking, in which a thousand British soldiers were 'imprisoned' by eight thousand Boers, ended on 17 May 1900. The commanding officer of the British forces was Robert Baden-Powell, who went on to found the Boy Scout Movement in 1908.

The Moa bird of New Zealand, which became extinct four hundred years ago, was over ten feet tall.

The Inca emperors were benevolent dictators, and made sure that no one went hungry or unclothed.

A manned rocket can reach the moon in less time than it used to take to travel the length of England by stagecoach.

The Star of David was never used as a religious symbol by the Ancient Israelites.

MAY (18)

Bertrand Russell, the English philosopher who was born today in 1872, was a prominent member of the original Campaign for Nuclear Disarmament. He was arrested and put-in prison after a demonstration in 1961 at the age of eighty-nine, and was still actively campaigning for peace well into his nineties.

Rye grass can put out roots measuring hundreds of miles.

The French poet, J.-A. Rimbaud, gave up poetry at the age of nineteen, to live in a harem in Ethiopia.

During the fifteenth century, sick people were often dressed in red and surrounded by red objects because it was thought to help them get better.

Someone suffering from coprolalia has an uncontrollable desire to be foul-mouthed.

MAY (19)

Anne Boleyn, the fated second wife of King Henry VIII, was executed on 19 May 1536. It seems she had a most extraordinary body, with six fingers on one of her hands and three breasts.

In Ancient Greece, a woman's age was counted from the day of her marriage.

The books of the research libraries in New York are arranged solely according to their height.

Eighty per cent of all body heat escapes through the head.

Sahara means 'desert' in Arabic.

MAY (20)

Christopher Columbus, the Italian explorer who is credited with the discovery of America, died on this day in 1506. On one occasion when he was in trouble with the inhabitants of Jamaica, and was in danger of losing his life, Columbus saved himself by blotting out the moon. He was able to perform this 'amazing' feat because he knew it was the date of a lunar eclipse.

Jesus was born in the reign of Herod, and it is known that Herod died in 4 BC. This means that Jesus was also born 'before Christ'. The mistake in dating was made in the sixth century, and has remained ever since.

Composer Johann Sebastian Bach once walked 230 miles to hear the organist at Lubeck in Germany.

It is illegal to drive a horse-drawn carriage in the City of London without a dispensation.

MAY (21)

The English satirical poet Alexander Pope was born on 21 May 1688. He grew to be only four feet six inches tall.

Sergei Prokofiev composed an opera called 'The Giant' when he was only seven years old.

Until 1999, Neptune is the planet farthest from the sun, not Pluto.

The blood of a grasshopper is not red, but white.

America kept 'burning at the stake' as a form of legal execution up to the beginning of the nineteenth century.

Two Prime Ministers — Winston Churchill and Clement Atlee — were taught by the same governess.

MAY (22)

Sir Arthur Conan Doyle, the writer who invented the famous detective, Sherlock Holmes, was born on this day in 1859. While officiating at the 1908 Olympics in London, Conan Doyle felt compelled to help a struggling Italian (who was leading at the time) over the finishing line in the Marathon. Unfortunately, such an action is against the rules and the runner was disqualified.

The United States, which accounts for six per cent of the population of the world, consumes nearly sixty per cent of the world's resources.

Like most Elizabethan playwrights, Christopher Marlowe had his plays printed anonymously.

Mary, Queen of Scots, displayed a ghoulish streak by having a watch made in the shape of a skull.

MAY 23

Pope Paul IV, who was elected on this day in 1555, was so outraged when he saw the naked bodies on the ceiling of the Sistine Chapel that he ordered Michelangelo to paint clothes on to them.

The Black Death claimed roughly forty million lives in the thirteenth century.

Before 1970, French families were not free to call their children just any old name, but had to choose one from the official government list.

Golden toads are so rare that a biological reserve has been specially created for them.

Thomas Gray, the English poet who wrote the popular 'Elegy in a Country Churchyard', refused to become Poet Laureate in 1757.

MAY 24

Bob Dylan, the American musician, was born on 24 May 1941. Though there is a poetry course devoted to his lyrics at Cambridge University, Dylan prefers to call himself a 'trapeze artist' rather than a poet. And when someone asked him what his songs were about, he replied: 'Some of them are about ten minutes long, others five or six.'

Cutting down a tree was a hanging offence in Britain until 1819.

When in 1816, the poets Byron and Shelley, their friend Dr Polidori, and Shelley's wife Mary, all agreed to write a ghost story each while on holiday in Switzerland, it was the least famous of the quartet, Mary Shelley, who came up with the goods. Her novel was published under the title **Frankenstein**.

The walking catfish can live on land.

MAY (25)

World heavyweight boxing champion, Gene Tunney, was born on 25 May 1898. He was not only one of the greatest boxers of all time, successfully defending his title on three occasions, but he also lectured on Shakespeare at the prestigious Yale University later in his life.

The temperature of the planet Mars can go as high as eighty degrees Fahrenheit during the day, and as low as minus one hundred and ninety degrees at night.

Thomas Crapper, a toilet salesman from London, wrote an autobiography entitled **Flushed With Pride**.

One thousand two hundred students streaked simultaneously in Boulder, Colorado, on 16 March 1974.

In 1929, Russia decreed that a week should forthwith consist of only five days. By 1940, however, the normal seven-day week had been restored.

MAY (26)

George Formby, the extremely popular English singer who was born today in 1904, was once awarded the Order of Lenin by Russia.

A pig was executed by public hanging in 1386 for the murder of a child.

The annual harvest of an entire coffee tree is needed to produce just one pound of coffee.

The tuna fish never stops moving in the water, and can swim millions of miles in its lifetime.

During the early nineteenth century, people used to inhale nitrous oxide (or 'laughing gas') to get high at parties.

MAY (27)

The Italian violin virtuoso, Nicolo Paganini, died on 27 May 1840. He was reputed to have had a hand-spread which measured a staggering eighteen inches.

Sir Walter Raleigh's widow carried his embalmed head around in a bag until her death.

It costs the West German Government over half a million pounds a year to keep Nazi war criminal, Rudolf Hess, in Spandau Gaol.

The earliest recorded circumnavigation of the British Isles occurred in 325 BC, and was achieved by a Greek called Pytheas.

Napoléon Bonaparte's wife could move her ears at will, and even turn them inside out.

MAY (28)

Ian Fleming, the creator of James Bond, was born on this day in 1908. Though his famous secret agent could never be called a saint, there is a church in Toronto, Canada called the St James Bond United Church.

Fried mice were once used to cure smallpox in Britain.

You are not allowed to eat snakes on a Sunday in Iraq.

Anyone stupid enough to refer to Czar Paul I's baldness was immediately flogged to death.

There are about eight miles of roads on the main island of the Isles of Scilly, but only one petrol station.

MAY (29)

Sir Edmund Hillary and Sherpa Tensing finally reached the summit of Mount Everest on 29 May 1953. Though these two men tend to get all the praise for this great achievement, they were helped on the climb by twelve other climbers, forty Sherpa guides, and over seven hundred porters.

After nuclear tests in the Sahara Desert, it was discovered that scorpions can withstand about two hundred times the amount of radiation which would kill a human being.

The Grand Inquisitor of the Spanish Empire, who had more than forty thousand people burnt at the stake, was canonized in 1860.

Ernest Hemingway, who won the Nobel Prize for Literature in 1954, gave his prize money to The Shrine of The Virgin in Cuba.

MAY (30)

Joan of Arc was declared a witch and burnt at the stake on 30 May 1431. In 1455, Charles VII, the man who had initially given her over to the ruthless church inquisitors, had the case re-opened. After Joan's family had been allowed to introduce new evidence, the previous verdict was quashed — albeit a little late. She eventually became Saint Joan in 1920.

If they were not married by the age of thirty, Spartan men not only lost the right to vote but were also banned from the popular nude parties.

Some toads and frogs use their eyeballs to force food from their mouths into their stomachs.

Catherine the Great's coronation procession from St Petersburg to Moscow contained over two hundred sleighs.

Camel-hunting is illegal in Arizona.

MAY (31)

Franz Joseph Haydn, the composer who died on 31 May 1809, taught Beethoven harmony when the great man was still a student. However, like many others, he failed to recognize his talent and advised Beethoven to give up music.

Twenty tons of raw materials must be mined each year to keep the inhabitants of America supplied with both necessities and luxuries.

About one hundred people die every minute, but over two hundred are born.

There is only one whole number that can be added to itself, and multiplied with itself, and still produce the same result — two.

JUNE

The Mormon religion allows polygamy. Brigham Young, who founded the Salt Lake City centre in 1847, had at least 20 wives.

I have good reason to remember 25 June 1950. That's the day the North Korean army took it into their heads to cross the 38th parallel and invade South Korea, giving me a return ticket to the war that followed. (Almost exactly a year later, on 23 June 1951, they were back to square one and settling for a cease-fire.)

JUNE 1

The Mormon leader, Brigham Young, who founded the religious centre in Salt Lake City in 1847, was born on 1 June 1801. The Mormon religion allows polygamy, and Brigham Young himself had at least twenty wives.

Burt Lancaster turned down the chance to play the lead in 'Ben Hur'. The film went on to win eleven Oscars, including one for Lancaster's replacement, Charlton Heston.

The average human male can produce five hundred million sperms in one ejaculation. The average horse produces sixteen times as much.

The most common surname in Germany is Schultz.

Over the years, the Niagara Falls have moved seven miles back upstream from their original site.

JUNE 2

Queen Elizabeth II was crowned on 2 June 1953. This particular day was chosen because meteorologists said it would be the most consistently sunny day of the year. It rained.

Dr Benjamin Spock, author of the best-selling book, **The Commonsense Book of Baby and Child Care**, was a member of the American rowing team at the 1924 Paris Olympics.

British hangman, Albert Pierrepoint, once had the unpleasant task of putting to death a friend from his local pub.

Edward VII had a private brothel on the Isle of Rum, just off the West Coast of Scotland.

A crow once built a nest made from barbed wire.

JUNE (3)

On 3 June 1956, a momentous historic event occurred which was destined to change the face of life in Britain — third-class railway travel was abolished.

A six-pound sea-hare can lay forty thousand eggs in a single minute.

The man who gave his name to Moet et Chandon's most famous vintage — Dom Perignon — was a blind Benedictine monk.

At a steady walking pace, you could walk the circumference of the earth in exactly one year.

The American lawyer involved in the extradition of a suspected Irish terrorist from the USA, was called Ira H. Bloch.

JUNE (4)

The adventurer, Giacomo Casanova, who is often called the world's greatest lover, died on this day in 1798. Although he was to go on to sleep with hundreds of women and cause scandals throughout Europe, he began his life by taking minor orders in the Church.

The Crown Jewels were kept in Aberystwyth during World War Two.

In the eighteenth century, fashionable people wore false eyebrows made out of mouse skin.

The father of George III, Frederick, died after being hit by a cricket ball.

The number of children born in India each year (about twelve million) is equal to the entire population of Australia.

JUNE 5

On 5 June 1783, the first hot-air balloon was invented. It was made of nothing more robust than paper.

In 1797, James Heatherington was fined £50 for wearing a top hat in public, after women had complained of being terrified by such a sight.

Many Oriental babies have a bruise mark on their bottoms until the age of two.

Abbad El Motaddid had an unusual taste in flower pots — he used the skulls of his enemies.

A special section of the Amsterdam police force has been set up to deal with motorists who get stuck in one of the city's canals.

JUNE 6

Jeremy Bentham, the English political reformer who devised the theory of Utilitarianism, died on 6 June 1832. He gave the whole of his large estate to University College Hospital, London, on the condition that he be stuffed and allowed to sit in on all future board meetings. His wish was granted, and the tradition continued for ninety-two years.

Shakespeare left no words of actual autobiography.

In 1978, the United Nations food and agricultural organization estimated that 'all the tea in China' amounted to 356,000 metric tons.

Yugoslavia has seven neighbouring countries which touch its borders — Italy, Austria, Hungary, Bulgaria, Romania, Albania, and Greece.

JUNE (7)

Beau Brummel, the dandy who dictated fashion trends in the first part of the nineteenth century, was born today in 1778. When he got older, he lost his place in high society and was imprisoned for debt. He eventually died a pauper in a lunatic asylum at the age of sixty-two.

Ulysses S. Grant was the first American President to visit China in the nineteenth century.

In 1354, many people died during a three-day fight between students and 'townies' in Oxford.

Eric the Red named the country covered in ice which he discovered in the tenth century, Greenland, in order to encourage settlers.

The composer John Cage's piece, 'Imaginary Landscape No. 4', is scored for twelve radios tuned at random.

JUNE (8)

The prophet Mohammed died on 8 June 632. Though he thought dogs were unclean, he had a deep respect for cats, and once cut off his sleeve so as not to disturb a sleeping cat as he was getting up.

Lord Nelson asked to be buried in St Paul's Cathedral, because he had heard that Westminster Abbey was sinking into the Thames.

The mathematician Cardano was imprisoned for doing a horoscope of Jesus Christ.

In our galaxy, there are five billion stars bigger than the Sun.

The inhabitants of Moscow (and their visitors) eat more than one hundred and seventy tons of ice-cream a day, winter and summer alike.

JUNE 9

Charles Dickens, who died on this day in 1870, was an insomniac. He believed that he had the best chance of getting some sleep if he positioned himself exactly in the middle of the bed, which must at all times be pointing in a northerly direction.

The philosopher Descartes speculated that monkeys could in fact speak, but that they chose not to in order to avoid having to work.

The actor, Stewart Granger, changed his name because he didn't like his real name, James Stewart.

Every year in France there is a 'Thieves' Fair', where people are encouraged to try to steal things from the stalls — if they think they can get away with it.

JUNE 10

The great American singer and actress, Judy Garland, was born today in 1922. Her original name was the distinctly unglamorous Frances Gumm.

Over twenty-five thousand people lost their lives during the construction of the Panama Canal.

In 1924, an eighteen-foot-high candle weighing three tons was erected in honour of the singer, Enrico Caruso, in Naples.

The composer of the French revolutionary song, 'The Marseillaise', had once been a strong royalist.

JUNE (11)

The Formula One driver, Jackie Stewart, was born on this day in 1939. Not only has he won three motor racing world championships, but he has also been British champion clay pigeon shooter on no fewer than five occasions.

Eccentric millionaire, Howard Hughes, was known as 'Saddlebags' when he got older, because of all the loose skin on the lower half of his body.

If the present birth rate continues, New York will have a black majority by the end of the century.

Nineteenth-century US President, Andrew Johnson, was a slave as a child.

On average there was a church for every two hundred people during the high Middle Ages.

JUNE (12)

Thomas Arnold, who died on 12 June 1842, was headmaster of Rugby School at the time of the now famous 'handball' incident. During a game of football, a pupil decided to pick up the ball and run towards the opposition's line. This breach of the rules gave rise to the formation of a whole new game — Rugby.

The female angler-fish weighs up to half a ton. The male, however, is only a few millimetres long, and spends his whole life attached to her nose.

George Bernard Shaw rejected the Order of Merit.

Within a few years of Columbus' discovery of America, the Spaniards had killed one and a half million Indians.

The bloodhound is the only animal whose evidence is admissable in an American court.

JUNE (13)

William Butler Yeats, who was born on 13 June 1865, is considered one of the greatest poets of the twentieth century, yet he wrote his most important poems between the age of fifty and seventy-five.

If they all lived, two ordinary house flies could produce 5,000,000,000,000 offspring in one season.

Gandhi slept with naked women in order to test his mastery of celibacy.

When Queen Christina of Sweden was forced to marry the impotent Duke of Cadiz, she spent their wedding night with one of the palace guards.

JUNE (14)

Hawaii officially became part of the United States on 14 June 1900. Hawaii's Mount Waialeale is the wettest place in the world — it rains about ninety per cent of the time, producing an annual rainfall of about 480 inches.

William the Conqueror's body was left to fester for a week after his death, so that it burst as it was being placed in its coffin.

If the population of China walked past you in single file, the line would never end because of the rate of reproduction.

In seventeenth-century Holland, the tulip was a major commodity, often fetching high prices at auction.

The inhabitants of Iceland are probably the most literate people in the world, reading more books per capita than any other country.

JUNE 15

The Magna Carta was 'signed' on 15 June 1215 at Runnymede. King John didn't actually put his name to the document because he couldn't read or write, so he had to place his seal on it instead.

The 'Sermon on the Mount' was proclaimed as seditious literature by a magistrate during World War One.

In 1562 a man was dug up six hours after his burial, after he had been seen to be breathing. He lived for another seventy-five years.

A scorpion could survive for three weeks if it was embedded in a block of ice.

Doctors 'bled' Louis XIII of France forty-seven times in one month in an attempt to cure his illness.

JUNE 16

Burglars were arrested in the Watergate building of the Democratic Party headquarters on 16 June 1972, beginning one of the worst scandals in the history of American politics. Richard Nixon, who many saw as the guilty party, suffered greatly in the ensuing enquiries, and eventually he resigned as President. Between 1970 and 1978, a poll was carried out in Madame Tussaud's waxworks in London, which asked people who they hated most in the world. Richard Nixon came third, behind Adolf Hitler, but ahead of Dracula.

Mary Stuart became Queen of Scotland at the tender age of six days.

Alexander the Great was tutored by the eminent Greek thinker, Aristotle.

There are more nutrients in the cornflake packet itself than there are in the actual cornflakes.

JUNE (17)

June 17 was not only the date of birth of King John III of Poland but was also the date of his coronation, his marriage, and ultimately his death.

After winning 100,000 francs in a State lottery, Claude Monet was at last able to pursue his lifelong ambition of painting the countryside.

Knowledge is growing so fast that ninety per cent of what we will know in fifty years' time, will be discovered in those fifty years.

After his sight improved, Thomas Edison still preferred using Braille to more normal reading.

The American athlete, Ray Ewry, who won three gold medals at the 1900 Olympic Games, had been paralysed and confined to a wheelchair as a child. He won all his medals for jumping events.

JUNE (18)

The Battle of Waterloo was fought today in 1815, though the actual battlefield was some miles away from the British headquarters at Waterloo. In England, after the victory, 'Waterloo teeth' were sold as mementoes from the battle, having been ripped from the unfortunate French corpses.

Alexander Graham Bell, the man who invented the telephone, also set a world water-speed record of over seventy miles an hour at the age of seventy-two.

The major export of Liechtenstein is false teeth.

The average qualification gained by children at school in this country is CSE grade four.

Shoe sizes were once measured in barleycorns.

JUNE (19)

James I of England, who was born today in 1566, gave cannabis plants to each settler in Jamestown, Virginia.

Queen Victoria inadvertently caused the death of her beloved Albert when the effluent pipe from her chamber burst, flooding his with dirty, disease-ridden water.

In 1908 the Moskva River in Russia rose nine metres, flooding 100 streets and 2,500 houses.

The book by Copernicus which suggested that the Sun, not the Earth, was the centre of the Solar System, was officially banned as heretical by the Papacy until 1835.

If eighty per cent of your liver was removed, it could still function, and would eventually restore itself to its original state.

JUNE (20)

On 20 June 1756, 146 British men and women were locked in a small guardroom measuring fifteen feet by eighteen, in the Indian city of Calcutta. Only twenty-three people survived the ordeal, which became known as the 'Black Hole of Calcutta'.

Ben Johnson once killed another actor in a duel, but was let off any charge because he could read and write, and was therefore able to claim 'right of clergy'.

Beethoven originally dedicated his third symphony to Napoléon, but withdrew the honour after learning of Napoléon's decision to take the title of Emperor.

There is about two hundred times as much gold dissolved in the world's oceans than has been mined in our entire history.

JUNE (21)

Friedrich Froebel, the German educationalist, died on this day in 1852. His revolutionary idea of the **Kindergarten** did not find favour during his lifetime, and was in fact banned until eight years after his death.

Queen Berengaria, the wife of Richard I of England, never set foot on English soil.

The first edition of The Gospels written in the language of the Eskimos was printed in Copenhagen in 1744.

An Englishman called Charles Wells broke the bank at Monte Carlo twelve times on his first visit there, becoming the subject of the famous Victorian song — 'The man who broke the bank at Monte Carlo'.

The founder of the Macdonald's hamburger chain is a Bachelor of Hamburgerology (BH).

JUNE (22)

On 22 June 1633, after threats of torture to himself and his family, Galileo was eventually forced to admit the falsehood of his astronomical theories — theories which now form the basis of our thinking. His tormentors were none other than the Papacy itself, who regarded the idea that the earth was not the centre of the universe as highly blasphemous.

In 1650, the body of Anne Green, who had been hanged for murder, was found to be still alive by the Anatomy Department of Oxford University, where it had been sent for research.

In November 1970, half a million people died when a tropical cyclone hit the Bay of Bengal and East Pakistan.

Not one new livestock animal has been domesticated in the last four thousand years.

JUNE (23)

On 23 June 1611, soon after he had discovered what later became known as Hudson River and Hudson Bay, the navigator Henry Hudson was cast adrift by his crew, and left to die. To this day no one knows exactly why the mutiny happened.

During World War Two, the Americans had the idea of fitting bats with miniature bombs which would then be dropped as they flew over the enemy.

Granada Television's long-running serial 'Coronation Street' was originally entitled 'Florizel Street'.

The scorpion fish can merge the shape of its head with the surrounding rocks.

There are more than eight thousand elks in the woods of Moscow's 'Green Belt'.

JUNE (24)

Henry Ward Beecher, who was a religious leader and divine, was born on 24 June 1813. In 1874 he was involved in a huge scandal when he was charged with adultery. Beecher claimed in court that God had willed him to have sex with the woman, and he was eventually acquitted.

Lime (or calcium oxide), when heated, produces a brilliant white light, and used to be employed to some effect to illuminate stages at the start of the century, hence the phrase 'to be in the limelight'.

You use up more calories in the action of eating a stick of celery than are contained in the stick itself.

The early Greeks experimented with the direction of their writing, going from right to left and left to right alternately, before adopting what is now the standard Western practice.

JUNE (25)

George Orwell, the Socialist writer who was born today in 1903, and who at one time was a tramp in both Paris and London, was educated at Eton.

Frank Lentini (known as the 'King of the Freaks') had three legs, four feet, sixteen toes, and two sets of genitals. His deformities were the result of his mother giving birth to non-separating triplets, but they did not stop him getting married and having four healthy children.

Leonardo da Vinci invented an alarm clock which woke the sleeper by gently rubbing his feet.

Though everyone thought he had been killed, Claudius was finally found by a palace guard hiding behind a curtain and crowned Emperor of Rome.

The plant life contained in the oceans of the world makes up eighty-five per cent of all our greenery.

JUNE (26)

Samuel Crompton, who died today in 1827, was the inventor of the very popular spinning mule. Because he couldn't afford to take out a patent on his invention, he only made £60 out of the whole operation.

When his wife Eleanor died, King Henry II had crosses built at every place that her body stopped on the journey to London for burial. The most famous is perhaps Charing Cross in London.

During the First World War, a sanitary policeman was placed outside each latrine to make sure the user covered up his excreta with earth.

The first time that a woman appeared on the stage completely nude was at the Folies-Bergère in Paris in 1912.

Mr Vroom is a motorcycle dealer in South Africa.

JULY (27)

On 27 June 1880, a girl called Helen Keller was born. She went on to graduate from university and write ten novels, a remarkable feat for someone who was both deaf and blind.

If you translate them literally, the Chinese words 'kung fu' mean 'leisure time'.

There are as many rats in Britain as people.

Until the end of the eighteenth century, lions were used to guard the Tower of London.

The ball-point pen was invented by two brothers — George and Lazlo Biro.

JUNE (28)

The French thinker, Jean Rousseau, who was born today in 1712, was adopted as a child. His foster mother used to beat him regularly until she discovered that he was enjoying it too much.

William the Conqueror was so strong that he could jump on to his horse wearing full armour.

The Indian atlas-moth has a twelve-inch wing span.

The Niagara Falls are switched off at night.

A kangaroo can only jump if its tail is touching the ground.

During the film 'Don Juan', John Barrymore delivers a grand total of 191 kisses to a variety of different women, at the rate of one every fifty-three seconds.

JUNE (29)

The oldest authenticated man in the world, Shigechiyo Izumi of Japan, was 118 years old on 29 June 1983.

On average you lose eleven ounces a night while you are sleeping.

Joseph Conrad, considered one of the greatest English writers of the twentieth century, was born in Poland, and couldn't speak a word of English until the age of forty-seven.

A female rhinoceros has to go through a pregnancy lasting 560 days.

Over a quarter of Russia is covered by forest.

JUNE (30)

Thomas Beddoes, the macabre English writer, was born on 30 June 1803. He wrote the gruesome **Death's Jest Book**, and in 1849 he ended his life in appropriate style by committing suicide.

There are more germs in the human mouth than the anus.

John Churchill, the first Duke of Marlborough, was allergic to cabbage.

There is more pigment in brown eyes than there is in blue eyes.

Her Majesty's Stationary Office issues two million rolls of 'hard' toilet paper to the Civil Service and Armed Forces each year.

JULY

Rather than kiss, the Samoans simply smell each other.

Henry Ford, born on 30 July 1863, probably had less impact on my life than many other people's in the Western world. In spite of appearing in cars in films and owning a car myself, I've never learned to drive. Fortunately, Shakira did. Better still, she doesn't mind taking the wheel when we're out together.

JULY 1

Allan Pinkerton, the American who founded the famous detective agency named after him in the early nineteenth century, died in rather strange circumstances on 1 July 1884. He stumbled, bit his own tongue, and was killed by the resulting gangrene.

Bald eagles are not really bald, they only seem to be.

Rather than kiss, the Samoans simply smell each other.

Nearly a quarter of all the bones in the human body can be found in the feet.

Sri Lanka is the second largest tea-producer in the world.

JULY 2

Betty Grable, the Hollywood actress who died on this day in 1973, was the most popular pin-up girl of the Second World War. Not only did her photograph hang inside most GIs' lockers, but it was also enlarged and used by the American Army for instruction in aerial map reading.

Soda water contains no soda.

There are over fifty distinct groups of Indians living in Mexico today.

Rhinoceros horn, which is much in demand for medicinal purposes, is not a horn at all, but is the animal's hair.

The Book of Solomon in The Bible was written long after he had died.

JULY (3)

On this day in 1976, Israeli commandoes carried out a raid on Entebbe Airport in Uganda, rescuing 103 people being held hostage by pro-Palestinian terrorists. Within a year, two films were on major release cashing in on the adventure.

It was not until two years after his death, that Oliver Cromwell was hanged and decapitated.

It is difficult to tell one end from the other of a stump-tailed lizard — its tail looks like its head.

At a steady walking pace, it would take about twelve hours to walk off a pound of fat.

King Richard the Lionheart only spent five per cent of his reign in England.

JULY (4)

Marie Curie, the Nobel Prize-winning scientist who discovered radium, fell foul of her own discovery when, on 4 July 1934, she died as a result of over-exposure to radioactivity.

Crocodiles can see underwater because they have a semi-transparent third eyelid which slides into place when necessary.

In 1972, a Swedish man balanced on one foot for over five hours, using nothing for support.

There is a Rocking Stone in Cornwall which, though it weighs many tons, can be rocked with ease.

Two-thirds of the body's weight is water.

JULY 5

The extraordinary circus impresario, Phineas T. Barnum, was born on 5 July 1810. His guiding philosophy in life was that 'There's a sucker born every minute', though it's not known whether he included himself in the generalization.

In nearly every language in the world, the word for mother begins with an 'm' sound.

The 'funny bone' in our elbow is not a bone at all, but a nerve.

The greater dwarf lemur in Madagascar always gives birth to triplets.

Costa Rica hasn't got an army.

JULY 6

On 6 July 1535, Sir Thomas More was beheaded for refusing to give his blessing to the divorce of King Henry VIII and his first wife Catherine of Aragon. As he rested his head on the chopping block, Sir Thomas moved his beard to one side with the words, 'This at least hath not offended the King'.

William Shakespeare had eleven different ways of spelling his surname.

Between 1930 and 1934, there was no such thing as a speed limit in Britain.

Some of the canals in Venice have traffic lights.

Leonardo da Vinci could draw with one hand and write with the other — at the same time.

JULY (7)

Gustave Mahler, the German musician who was born on 7 July 1860, has written the longest orchestral symphony of all time. His Symphony No. 3 in D Minor requires not only a full orchestra, but also a women's and boys' choir, and an organ. Performances can last at least an hour and a half.

Members of the House of Lords do not wear gloves in the presence of the Queen.

South Africa produces two-thirds of the world's gold.

Minus forty degrees centigrade is exactly the same as minus forty degrees Fahrenheit.

A frog's tongue starts growing from the front of its mouth, making it easier to catch insects.

JULY (8)

Horse-racing starting-stalls were only introduced to Britain on 8 July 1965, in the Chesterfield Stakes at Newmarket.

The Maoris in New Zealand used to tattoo their chins.

Darts is the most popular sport played in Britain.

Edward III passed a law stopping people eating more than two meals a day.

The volume of water in the Amazon is greater than the **combined** total of the next eight largest rivers in the world.

JULY 9

King Camp Gillette, the man who invented the first disposable safety razor, died on 9 July 1932. Two years after he first patented his invention, he had only sold 168 blades, but by the following year sales had jumped to an incredible 12.4 million blades.

The Mongolian wild horse is the only species of truly wild horse left in the world.

The tip of a Kiwi's beak is so sensitive that it can feel worms wriggling about deep underground.

A father cannot be charged with infanticide.

Israeli women are the only women in the world who must undergo compulsory military service.

JULY 10

Lady Jane Grey was proclaimed Queen of England on 10 July 1553 at the age of sixteen. She only lasted a grand total of nine days, before she was arrested and executed.

The Earth is the densest planet in our Solar System.

Yehudi Menhuin performed in public for the first time when only eight years old.

Denmark has the oldest national flag in the world.

People used to wear shoes on either foot.

JULY (11)

On 11 July 1962, Fred Baldsare became the first person to swim the English Channel **underwater**, using 'scuba' equipment.

If you're suffering from 'acute nasopharyngitis', you've got a cold.

A thick glass is more likely to crack if hot water is poured into it than a thin one.

There are people who are professional tea-tasters.

Mohammed, the founder of Islam, once called himself a 'Jewish Prophet'.

JULY (12)

The American writer, Henry Thoreau, was born on 12 July 1817. He was an extremely ugly man, and his nose was so long he could swallow it.

The legs of a giraffe will break very easily.

Chief Sitting Bull was a medicine man, and didn't join in the fighting at the Battle of Little Big Horn.

The American multi-millionaire, Jean Paul Getty, wrote a book called **How To Be Rich**.

JULY 13

On this very day in 1798, William Wordsworth wrote his famous 'lines composed a few miles above Tintern Abbey'. During his seven years as Poet Laureate later in his life, he didn't write any poetry.

In 1818, Thomas Bowdler published **The Family Shakespeare**, which rewrote the Bard's plays leaving out any words which he considered obscene.

The popular card game, Bridge, was invented in Turkey.

Baked beans were originally sold with treacle, not tomato sauce.

Nowhere in England is more than seventy-five miles from the sea.

JULY 14

Gerald Ford, who became President of America after the resignation of Richard Nixon, was born on 14 July 1913 as plain Leslie King Junior. He was well known for his gaffes, and once called Anwar Sadat the 'President of Israel'. Former President Lyndon B. Johnson summed up much of the criticism of Gerald Ford when he said that he 'is so dumb that he can't fart and chew gum at the same time'.

Every single one of Queen Anne's seventeen children died before she did.

A solar eclipse cannot last longer than seven minutes and fifty-eight seconds.

Shirley Temple was a dollar millionairess before the age of ten.

It is a Hindu custom not to cut a child's fingernails before they are one year old.

JULY (15)

On 15 July 1883, General Tom Thumb, probably the most famous midget of all time, died measuring only forty inches. On exactly the same day, fifty-seven years later, Robert Wadlow also died measuring a staggering one hundred and seven inches — he was the tallest man who ever lived.

It is possible to extract aspirin from the bark of some trees.

The Red Sea is never mentioned in the Bible.

King Edward VIII is the only British monarch to have written an autobiography.

African witch-doctors only send their patients a bill if they expect them to live.

JULY (16)

Hilaire Belloc, a writer of many talents, died on 16 July 1953. He had already written his own epitaph which read: 'When I am dead, I hope it may be said:/ "His sins were scarlet, but his books were read."'

The people of Eire drink more tea per capita than any other country in the world.

The Battle of Hastings wasn't fought at Hastings, but at Senlac Hill which is six miles away.

Rudolf Hess was locked up in the Tower of London during the Second World War.

The screwdriver was invented before the screw.

JULY (17)

James Cagney was born on this day in 1899. Though he is most famous for his many gangster films, he started his career as a chorus girl, and his studio publicized the year of his birth as 1904 in order to capitalize on his baby face.

Only the male nightingale sings.

Maurice Utrillo was already an alcoholic when he decided to start painting at the age of seventeen.

The population of the American colonies at the start of the sixteenth century was about three hundred and fifty.

Most people blink about 25,000 times a day.

JULY (18)

W.G. Grace, who was born on 18 July 1848, is thought by many people to have been the greatest cricketer of all time. He was also very talented at other sports, and on one occasion in 1866, after scoring 224 not out for England against Surrey on the two preceding days, he won the 440 yards hurdles at the first National Olympian Association meeting at Crystal Palace.

A chamelon's body is often only half the length of its tongue.

A tarantula, although a spider, cannot spin a web.

It is illegal for bees to make a buzzing noise in Ottawa, Canada.

England is smaller than New England in America.

JULY 19

Lizie Borden was born on 19 July 1860. At the age of thirty-two, and an apparently harmless spinster, she became involved in one of the most notorious murder cases in history when she was charged with hacking to death with an axe both her father and her stepmother. Many people thought that she was guilty of the crime, largely because she had predicted a family disaster a few days earlier, but the case was never proven; and Lizzie Borden was released.

George Sand wrote all her novels at night.

Julius Caesar was an epileptic.

It was the custom for seventeenth-century English ladies to wear their wedding ring on their thumb.

The United Nations has five official languages — Chinese, French, Spanish, Russian, and English.

JULY 20

The English Football Association Challenge Cup Competition was formed on 20 July 1871, to become better known over the years as the FA Cup. The first final saw the 'Wanderers' beat the 'Royal Engineers' by one goal to nil, watched by a crowd of only two thousand.

If you fly from London to New York by Concorde, you can arrive at your destination two hours before the time of your departure.

Lapland spreads across four different countries.

You can usually estimate an elephant's height by doubling the circumference of its foot.

The human body contains enough fat to produce seven bars of soap.

JULY (21)

On 21 July 1969, bookmakers paid out £10,000 to David Threlfall as Neil Armstrong became the first man to set foot on the moon. Mr Threlfall had wagered £10 at 1000-1 in 1964 that a man would set foot on the moon within seven years.

King Alexander of Greece died of blood poisoning in 1920, after he had been bitten by his pet monkey.

A black widow spider can devour as many as twenty 'husbands' in a single day.

King George VI competed at the Wimbledon tennis championships.

There are nearly four thousand species of beetle in Britain alone.

JULY (22)

Philip the Handsome of Spain was born on 22 July 1478. After his death his wife kept his corpse, and continued to sleep with it beside her in bed for three years. Her name was Joanna the Mad.

There are 602 rooms in Buckingham Palace.

Nearly a quarter of the population of Poland was killed in the Second World War.

There are no rivers in Saudi Arabia.

St John's Lane in Rome is only half a metre wide.

JULY (23)

Raymond Chandler, the detective writer who created the legendary Philip Marlowe, was born on this day in 1888. While Chandler was hard at work on his typewriter, his wife Cissy used to do the housework — in the nude.

It is not certain whether the Mexican chihuahua should be classified as a dog, or as a type of rodent.

Taiwan exports more mushrooms than any other country in the world.

Scientists have found that the number of UFO sightings increase at those times when Mars is nearest the Earth.

In Texas in the 1930s, the post of State Treasurer was held by a midget.

JULY (24)

The first man to swim the English Channel without a life jacket was Captain Matthew Webb. He completed the crossing in August 1875 in 21 hours 45 minutes. He died eight years later on 24 July 1883, as he was attempting another record by swimming the Rapids above the Niagara Falls.

An owl can turn its head in a complete circle.

The first city in the world to have a population of over one million was London.

The inspiration for Defoe's **Robinson Crusoe** was a sailor called Alexander Selkirk who spent four years alone on a desert island.

The Basque word for God is 'Jingo'.

JULY (25)

Samuel Taylor Coleridge, the romantic poet and critic who died on 25 July 1834, was in severe financial trouble as an undergraduate at university. So much so that he joined the army under the alias Silas Tomkyn Comerbache, but he was soon found out.

After a weekend at Sandringham, guests of Edward VII were weighed to see if they had eaten well.

Stalin, who was reponsible for a great deal of religious persecution in Russia, studied theology as a young man.

Our own galaxy is minute compared to the radio galaxies being discovered at the edge of the universe.

An oak tree over 100 feet high can grow from a one-inch long acorn.

JULY (26)

The British novelist, Aldous Huxley, was born on 26 July 1894. An illness during childhood left his sight seriously impaired, but he did not give up his ambition to be a writer, and actually learnt Braille in order to keep up with his reading.

The energy released in the ten minutes of a normal hurricane is roughly equivalent to the energy contained in all the nuclear stockpiles of the world.

A woodchuck breathes only ten times an hour during hibernation.

The human head is a quarter of our total length at birth, but only an eighth of our total length by the time we reach adulthood.

Michelangelo lived to the grand old age of eighty-eight.

JULY (27)

Vincent Van Gogh, who shot himself on this day in 1890 at the age of thirty-seven, was a painter whose greatness was only recognized after his tragic suicide. It is doubtful whether he sold more than one or two paintings in his whole lifetime.

It seems that goldfish actually get seasick every now and then.

The first coins minted in the United States were made from Martha Washington's silver service.

So far in the twentieth century, two objects have hit the earth's surface with enough force to destroy a medium-sized city. By pure luck, both have landed in sparsely populated Siberia.

At birth a panda weighs only four ounces, and is about the same size as a mouse.

JULY (28)

One of the greatest natural disasters of recent centuries occurred on this day in 1976, when an earthquake hit Tangshan in China, killing three-quarters of a million people.

The South American Incas had no natural supply of iron and, before the Spanish arrived in the fifteenth century, they used to make even the most mundane objects out of gold, including cutlery, combs, and nails.

England's Stonehenge is 1500 years older than Rome's Colosseum.

When they are young, Black Sea basses are mostly female, but at the age of five many switch sexes and are able to function satisfactorily as males.

JULY 29

The BBC put out the first televised weather forecast on 29 July 1949, though I have not been able to find out whether their prediction was right or wrong.

The Dead Sea is in fact an inland lake.

King George V was an avid stamp collector, and amassed over three hundred albums during his lifetime.

The men working on the tomb of Rameses III in the twelfth century BC went on strike in support of a pay claim.

Dirty snow melts quicker than clean snow.

JULY 30

Henry Ford, the famous car manufacturer who was born on 30 July 1863, subsidized an anti-Semitic newspaper and had a picture of Adolf Hitler on his desk.

Joseph Stalin smoked a pipe in public, but preferred cigarettes when on his own.

In 1896, Britain and Zanzibar were at war for only thirty-eight minutes.

From fertilization to birth, a baby's weight increases 5000 million times.

JULY (31)

On 31 July 1956, Jim Laker took all ten Australian wickets for just 53 runs in the second innings of the Old Trafford Test Match, having got figures of 9 for 37 in the first innings.

Phillipe, Duke of Orleans, was brought up as a woman, and used to lead his troops into battle wearing high heels.

Both Elvis Presley and his mother died when they were the same age — forty-two.

Ninety per cent of Indian girls are married by the age of twenty.

The Ainu women of Japan always cover their mouths with one of their hands when called on to speak to a man.

AUGUST

The choristers at the Vatican in Rome used to be castrated, until the practice was stopped at the end of the last century.

August 1954 marked a watershed in my life. You could almost say one life ended and another began; it certainly felt like it at the time.

I'd just been offered a walk-on part as a prison warder in Jean Anouilh's play 'The Lark', in which I had to take Joan of Arc out to her trial. The part itself wasn't a problem. My name was.

Equity got wind that I had been cast and contacted my agent to say that I couldn't call myself Michael Scott (my stage name by that time) because they already had one on their books. They said I couldn't call myself by my real name either. Amazingly, they also had a Maurice Micklewhite (the male line in our family had been called Maurice for three generations). If I wanted the part, I had to have another name and they gave me until six that evening to come up with one.

That left me eight hours to dream up a new identity, and I wandered miserably round the West End trying one option after another. None sounded right, and in the end I went into the Odeon, Leicester Square, where 'The Caine Mutiny' was showing.

Bogie came to my help again. Across the Square in a coffee bar after the film, I looked up at the neon title. The name 'Caine' hit me – and has stuck ever since.

AUGUST 1

Louis Blériot, the French aviator who died on 1 August 1936, was the first person to fly across the English Channel in 1909. The journey, which took thirty-six-and-a-half minutes, ended with Bleriot crash-landing his plane near Dover Castle.

The choristers at the Vatican in Rome used to be castrated, until the practice was stopped at the end of the last century.

Lucrezia Borgia had been married four times by the time she was twenty-two.

Lunar eclipses cannot occur more than three times a year.

Irving Berlin's 'White Christmas' has sold over one hundred million copies.

AUGUST 2

Enrico Caruso, the great Italian tenor, died on 2 August 1921. His recording of the aria 'Vesti La Giubba' from the opera 'I Pagliacci' by Leoncavallo was the earliest record to 'go gold' and achieve a total sale of one million copies.

More coffee is consumed per capita in Sweden than in any other country.

Until 1879, any British soldier found guilty of bad conduct was reminded of his misdemeanour by having the initials 'BC' tattooed on his body.

Russians are not allowed to own their own land.

The Battle of Hastings took place on King Harold's birthday.

AUGUST (3)

On 3 August 1492, Christopher Columbus left Spain on his historical voyage to the New World. The expedition was run on a shoestring budget, and the total cost in terms of today's money would be just under £4,000.

The first person to be buried in the prestigious Poet's Corner in Westminster Abbey was Geoffrey Chaucer.

The last dodo died in 1681.

There is a violent sect in India called the Thuggees.

India makes more films every year than any other country in the world.

AUGUST (4)

Hans Christian Andersen, the Danish writer most famous for his fairy tales, died on this day in 1875. He was very conscious of his pigeon chest, and used to stuff old newspapers under his shirt to pad out his figure, and make himself look more virile.

Glaciers cover about ten per cent of the earth's surface.

The average height of a man in the Middle Ages was five feet six inches.

A caterpillar has three times as many muscles in its body as a human being.

The actress, Sarah Bernhardt, often spent the night lying in a coffin.

AUGUST 5

Marilyn Monroe died after taking an overdose of sleeping pills on 5 August 1962. Her second husband, the baseball player Joe Dimaggio, has had fresh roses placed on her grave three times a week ever since.

The egg came before the chicken in the sense that reptiles were laying eggs long before the first bird appeared on the earth.

Men are ten times more likely to be colour-blind than women.

The word 'karate' means 'empty hand'.

Nearly fifty-five million people died as a result of World War Two.

AUGUST 6

On 6 August 1945, an American B29 bomber dropped an atom bomb on the Japanese city of Hiroshima, immediately pulverizing everything within a two-mile radius. One hundred thousand people died that day, and a similar number were killed off by the resulting radiation. The bomb itself had a rather misleading nickname — 'Little Boy'.

If you are forced to pay out a ransom to a kidnapper in America you can at least take comfort from the fact that the money is tax deductible.

Queen Victoria was a haemophilia carrier.

Alfred Lord Tennyson wrote a 60,000-word poem at the age of ten.

Milk is heavier than cream.

AUGUST 7

Oliver Hardy, the fat comedian who, with his partner Stan Laurel, formed one of the most successful double acts of all time, died on this day in 1957. Before teaming up with Laurel in 1926, Hardy had played many minor roles in films, and was especially in demand as a villain.

Birds can't fly much higher than 25,000 feet — which is about the height of Mount Everest.

The women of North Siberia show their affection by pelting the men with slugs.

Football was played in the twelfth century, though without any rules.

AUGUST 8

On 8 August 1963, one of the most daring crimes in British legal history occurred when the Glasgow to London Mail train was stopped at Sears Crossing, and robbed of over two-and-a-half million pounds. The incident became known as the Great Train Robbery, and the people responsible were instant celebrities. Though nearly all the men have now been caught, only £350,000 has been recovered.

All the New Testament writers were Jewish except St Luke.

The Ancient Egyptians believed that the Sacred Ibis was the bird which laid the 'world egg'.

According to an English chronicler, more knights were killed by a single lightning storm in 1360 than were killed at the Battles of Crécy and Poitiers.

Thomas Wedders, the English circus freak, had a nose which was seven-and-a-half inches long.

AUGUST 9

Gerald Ford was sworn in as the thirty-eighth President of the United States on this day in 1974. Though not the first Vice-President to succeed to the highest office in the land, he was the first President to serve without being chosen by the people in a national election.

Ice-hockey pucks travel at speeds of up to one hundred miles an hour.

You cannot be excommunicated from the Hindu religion.

One hundred and twenty drops of water are needed to fill a teaspoon.

AUGUST 10

Otto Lilienthal, the German aviator whose pioneering work made a significant contribution to the success of the Wright Brothers, died on 10 August 1896. Ironically, he was killed after his glider crashed.

In Spain, Sir Francis Drake is still seen as a 'bogey man', and is known by the nickname, 'The Dragon'.

The last British monarch to use the royal veto was Queen Anne in 1707.

Having a large fountain outside your house is a sign of great wealth in Morocco.

Hungary exports more hippopotamuses than any other country in Europe.

AUGUST (11)

The infamous Roderigo Borgia bribed enough cardinals to become Pope Alexander VI on this day in 1492. During his stay at The Vatican, this corrupt Pope openly enjoyed a series of mistresses, and was the father of several illegitimate children.

In the early days of the colony of Virginia, you could be executed for damaging or attempting to damage a tobacco plant.

Flamingos have to hold their heads upside down to eat.

Giraffes show their affection for each other by rubbing necks.

AUGUST (12)

Viscount Castlereagh committed suicide on 12 August 1822. He slit his throat with a rusty penknife after he was criticized for trying to dissolve the marriage of George IV and Queen Caroline.

The Ancient Greeks believed that boys developed in the right-hand side of the womb, and girls in the left.

The legs of Disraeli's bed were placed in bowls of salty water to ward off evil spirits.

Swami Maujgiri Maharij stood continuously for seventeen years as a penance.

Twice as many men as women commit suicide.

AUGUST (13)

The Cuban revolutionary leader, Fidel Castro, was born on 13 August 1926. The American CIA, desperate to undermine his popularity, once planned to put hair-remover inside his shoes during an overseas trip so that his famous beard would fall out.

Queen bees can lay three thousand eggs in just one day.

There is only one inanimate sign of the Zodiac — Libra.

Mexico once had three different Presidents in the space of twenty-four hours.

Louis XIV insisted that none of his courtiers sit in chairs with arms.

AUGUST (14)

On 14 August 1908, the first international beauty contest in Britain was held at the Pier Hippodrome in Folkestone, Kent.

We only put five per cent of the earth's plant life to any practical use.

Nero ate leeks to improve his singing voice.

The frankfurter originated in China.

An eighteenth-century woman who used only lard to 'wash' her face and hands lived to the age of 116.

AUGUST 15

T.E. Lawrence, popularly known as Lawrence of Arabia, was born on 15 August 1888. After he was raped and beaten by Turkish soldiers in 1917, he developed a taste for sado-masochism and used to pay an admirer (appropriately called John Birch) to whip him on the buttocks.

The French town of Bayonne gave its name to the bayonet.

The official name for Libya is the Socialist People's Libyan Arab Jamahiriya.

The cathedral in Milan took nearly six hundred years to build.

Iraq supplies three-quarters of the world's dates.

AUGUST 16

Bela Lugosi, the horror actor who became a drug addict later in his life, eventually died on 16 August 1956. He was buried (as he wished) in his famous 'Dracula' cape.

There are six million trees in The Forest of Martyrs near Jerusalem, symbolizing the Jewish death toll in World War Two.

Rubber is an important ingredient in the manufacture of bubble-gum.

In Wales, sheep outnumber people by nearly two to one.

There are prehistoric lizards still living on the Indonesian island of Komodo..

AUGUST (17)

Mae West, the legendary Hollywood actress, was born on this day in 1892. She was not afraid to flaunt her sensuality openly and could be said to have perfected the art of sexual innuendo. As she once put it: 'When I'm good I'm very, very good, but when I'm bad I'm better.'

The Incas and the Aztecs were able to function without the wheel.

Sir William Blackstone wrote perhaps the most influential book ever on English law, yet never practised law himself.

There are no 'roads', only 'streets', in the City of London.

Human adults breathe about 23,000 times a day.

AUGUST (18)

On 18 August 1587, seven days after Raleigh's second expedition landed, the first child to be born of English parents in the New World was delivered to a couple in North Carolina.

The Arctic tern flies to the Antarctic and back every year.

There is enough petrol in a full tank of a Jumbo Jet to drive an average car four times round the world.

The door to 10 Downing Street, home of Britain's Prime Minister, only opens from the inside.

Seventy-five per cent of the inhabitants of Norway live within ten miles of the sea.

AUGUST 19

The American comedian, Groucho Marx, died today in 1977. Though he freely admitted to making a fortune out of insulting people, he was a very popular man and, as Irving Berlin put it, 'The world would not be in such a snarl/if Marx had been Groucho instead of Karl.'

Every continent in the world contains a city called Rome.

If a woman commits adultery in the Tupuri tribe of Africa, she is forced to wear a brass ring round her neck for the rest of her life.

Half the world exists on a basic diet of rice.

Most mammals are colour-blind.

AUGUST 20

On 20 August 1940, a man entered the study of Leon Trotsky in his heavily fortified villa in Mexico, and smashed him on the head with an ice axe. The resulting three-inch wound proved to be fatal, and Trotsky died twenty-six hours later. His killer, who was probably put up to it by Trotsky's arch-enemy Joseph Stalin, was arrested and sentenced to twenty years in gaol.

Snow has fallen on London on Christmas Day only seven times since the start of the century.

The word 'girl' appears only once in the Bible.

The American poet, Emily Dickinson, used to talk to visitors from an adjoining room, because she was so self-conscious about her appearance.

Some Kenyans live **inside** the trunks of the baobab trees.

AUGUST (21)

On 21 August 1911, a Louvre employee called Vincenzo Peruggia stole the famous 'Mona Lisa' by Da Vinci. He kept it in a trunk for two years, and was eventually arrested when he tried to sell the painting to the Italian Government. Peruggia only received a one-year sentence after he convinced the court that he stole the masterpiece so that it could return to its country of origin.

Oliver Cromwell's real name was Oliver Williams.

The Chinese wear white at funerals.

There is a gypsy convention every year at Saintes-Maries-de-la-Mer in France.

The Bank of England has its own independent water supply.

AUGUST (22)

The American writer, Dorothy Parker, was born on this day in 1893. In 1950 she remarried her husband, Alan Campbell, after they had been divorced for three years. When someone at the reception remarked that some of the guests hadn't spoken to one another for years, Parker immediately quipped, 'Including the bride and groom'.

There is a delicatessen for dogs in New York.

Carrots are used as a substitute for coffee in Germany.

The male silkworm moth can smell a female over a distance of up to five miles.

There is an underpass across the M5 motorway near Exeter which was built for the exclusive use of badgers.

AUGUST (23)

Rudolph Valentino died from a perforated ulcer on 23 August 1926. Though many people think that he was a homosexual, thousands of women lined his funeral route, and there was rioting as the coffin was carried past.

The word 'school' comes from an old Greek word meaning 'leisure'.

The Russian writer Dostoyevsky once received a last-minute reprieve from the scaffold.

A wren can sing a hundred different notes in just a few seconds.

An Alsatian's sense of smell is a million times better than a man's.

AUGUST (24)

An Irish adventurer with the wonderful name of Captain Blood died on 24 August 1680. He achieved instant fame in 1671, when he made an unsuccessful attempt to steal the Crown Jewels from the Tower of London.

When people first started sending letters in Britain, it was the recipient who paid the postage.

An Australian fisherman once caught a new fishing rod.

Turtles don't have any teeth.

It takes sixty seconds for blood to make one complete circuit of the human body.

AUGUST (25)

Sean Connery, the Scottish actor who played James Bond so successfully for many years, was born today in 1930. Before he made his fortune in the film business, he had a variety of jobs, including one as a coffin-polisher.

Sir Winston Churchill was a prisoner-of-war during the Boer War.

The idea of Santa Claus as a fat, old man with white hair and whiskers, and dressed in a red suit, was invented by a nineteenth-century American artist.

The first car registration plate (A1) went to the second Earl of Russell.

Magnetic ants are so-called because they always build their nests pointing north and south.

AUGUST (26)

The actor, Lon Chaney, died on 26 August 1930. Known as the 'Man of a Thousand Faces', he invariably played monsters or outcasts from society, but always made his characters seem sympathetic and somehow vulnerable. Interestingly, he had some first-hand experience of the pain of disability, since both his parents were deaf-mutes.

It is the larvae of moths which can damage clothes, not the moths themselves.

The first victim of the electric chair took eight minutes to die.

Camel meat is a great delicacy in Egypt.

Stephen II was Pope only for two days.

AUGUST (27)

Hollywood film producer Sam Goldwyn was born on this day in 1882, though his original name was Samuel Goldfish. He had a no-nonsense approach to film-making and once said: 'What we want is a story that starts with an earthquake and works its way up to a climax.'

The first atomic power station was built in Russia in 1954.

The chemist who discovered barbituric acid named it after his wife Barbara.

Typewriters were originally conceived as an aid to the blind.

It seems that the most popular time for dying in the United States is in the first two months of the year.

AUGUST (28)

Johann Wolfgang von Goethe, one of the few writers who is mentioned in the same breath as Shakespeare, was born on 28 August 1749. In 1867, thirty-five years after his death, the first part of his masterpiece **Faust** became the first paperback book to go on sale in the world.

Over twenty million Africans were transported to America and the Caribbean during the three hundred years of the slave trade.

Ostrich-racing is a popular sport in South Africa.

Hammerfest in Norway is the most northerly town in the world.

The old 'X' certificate rating for films was introduced to Britain in 1951.

AUGUST 29

The Swedish actress, Ingrid Bergman, was born on 29 August 1915, and died on the same day in 1982. She caused a major scandal in Hollywood in 1951 when she gave birth to a child by the married Italian film director, Roberto Rossellini, and it took several years before she was forgiven by the American public.

It became fashionable for fourteenth-century French ladies to wear corsets over their normal clothes.

Half of all the different types of flowers in the world can be found in South America.

Harrow, the English Public School which is so steeped in tradition, once appointed a twenty-six-year-old headmaster.

The Japanese often spend hours soaking themselves in their public swimming pools.

AUGUST 30

King Louis XI of France died on this day in 1483. He once commanded one of his abbots to invent a new and ridiculous musical instrument for the amusement of the Court. The abbot gathered together a series of pigs, each with their own distinctive squeal, and proceeded to prick each of them in turn to provide the desired tune.

The world's first parking meters were installed in Oklahoma in 1935.

Henry I decided that 'a yard' should be the distance from his thumb to the end of his nose.

The colour purple was a sign of great rank in Ancient Rome.

149

AUGUST 31

The Roman Emperor Caligula, whose nickname was 'Little Boots', was born on 31 August AD 12. To say that he was an eccentric would be one of the understatements of history. At the age of twenty-five, he made himself a god, and his horse a senator.

The nail on the thumb grows the slowest of all.

A butterfly has 12,000 eyes.

The most common disease in the world is tooth decay.

The game of tennis originated in the French monastries of the eleventh century.

SEPTEMBER

Ice-cream was invented in 1620.

I was six when the Second World War broke out. On 3 September itself I was being evacuated to Wargrave in Berkshire with my mother and younger brother, Stan.

The war gave me freedom, as it must have done for masses of other kids. And, appropriately for this book, it made me appreciate playing-space. In Wargrave, we lived in the house right next to the recreation ground. Later, when we were evacuated to Norfolk, there were miles and miles of fields in which to run around and explore with the kids from the village.

Going back to London and a prefab (our pre-war home had been blitzed) was like going back to prison. The war taught me to value space and open air. I've never forgotten that.

SEPTEMBER (1)

Pope Adrian IV died on 1 September 1159. His real name was Nicholas Breakspear, and he is the only Englishman ever to become the head of the Roman Catholic Church.

Ice-cream was invented in 1620.

Ladybirds aren't birds at all — they're beetles.

Snakes have their hearing equipment in their jaws.

The Salvation Army's motto is 'Blood and fire'.

SEPTEMBER (2)

On this day in 1666, The Great Fire of London began at the bakery of Thomas Farriner in Pudding Lane. Though an enormous amount of property was burnt, only six people actually died.

Peter Labellière had himself buried upside down when he died because he thought the world was topsy-turvy.

The Japanese Santa Claus is a woman.

The average man will spend about 145 days of his life shaving.

Mozart wrote the music for the scng, 'Twinkle Twinkle, Little Star', when he was only five years old.

SEPTEMBER (3)

The film actor, Alan Ladd, was born on 3 September 1913. Though only five feet six inches tall, he made his name playing mean and moody cowboys, and was the first to speak the immortal lines: 'A man's gotta do what a man's gotta do.'

George Washington was the first person to wear false teeth.

There are no telephones in Greenland.

If you cut open the stomach of a grebe, you would find that half its contents were feathers.

Marco Polo brought spaghetti back from China.

SEPTEMBER (4)

Albert Schweitzer, who won the Nobel Prize for Peace in 1952, died on this day in 1965. He began his work as a missionary in French Equatorial Africa in 1913, but was arrested as a suspected German spy during World War One and put in prison in France.

The breed of dog we call the Great Dane originated in Germany, not Denmark.

The first letter of Christ's name in Greek is 'X' — hence the abbreviation 'Xmas'.

Robert Louis Stevenson wrote **Travels on a Donkey** during his honeymoon.

You can't arrest a Peer of the British Realm for a civil offence.

SEPTEMBER (5)

Louis XIV of France, the 'Sun King', was born on 5 September 1638. He had an unfortunate experience once while putting on a sock — his toe fell off.

The human stomach can only hold about five pints.

There are over five hundred different species of water-bug in England.

Camels' humps do not contain water, they contain fat.

Rice paper is not made from rice.

SEPTEMBER (6)

Ferdinand Magellan's ship, the **Vittoria**, under the command of Del Canio, arrived back in Spain on 6 September 1522 after completing the first circum-navigation of the world. Unfortunately, Magellan himself was not there to witness the historic event — he had been killed on the island of Mactan in the Philippines.

Most people change their sleeping position at least twenty times a night.

Turkish baths were invented by the Romans.

The Chinese were the first people to use wallpaper.

The Pont Neuf in Paris isn't new at all. In fact, it's one of the oldest bridges in the city.

SEPTEMBER 7

On this day in 1892, 'Gentleman' Jim Corbett beat J.L. Sullivan in twenty-one rounds to become the first world heavyweight boxing champion under the new Queensbury rules. They stipulated that gloves had to be worn, and that each round should last exactly three minutes.

Haggis was invented by the Ancient Greeks.

Ninety per cent of the human heart is on the right side of the body.

Bats are not blind.

The Virgin Mary is the subject of twice as many biographies as Jesus.

SEPTEMBER 8

King Richard I of England was born on this day in 1157. He never once slept with his wife and, according to some chroniclers, he kept a supply of prisoners at his disposal so that he could eat them if his food supplies ran low while at war.

Magnesium becomes heavier after it has been burned.

There is a town in West Virginia, USA, called Looneyville.

Elephants are not able to jump into the air.

The novel **Les Misérables** by Victor Hugo contains the longest sentence ever published. It's 823 words long.

157

SEPTEMBER (9)

When William the Conqueror died on 9 September 1087, he was buried at Rouen in France. In 1562, vandals broke into his tomb and stole everything but his thighbone, but during the French revolution, that too was taken.

Vaughan Williams, the English classical composer, once wrote a concerto for the mouth-organ.

Cleopatra's Needle, the obelisk situated on the Victoria Embankment in London, was built over fourteen centuries before the birth of Cleopatra.

American Indians used to barter for goods with the scalps of woodpeckers.

Mayflies only live for a matter of a few hours.

SEPTEMBER (10)

On 10 September 1897, a taxi-driver called George Smith became the first motorist in England to be convicted for drunken driving.

The game of marbles was introduced to Britain by the Romans.

It is very unlikely that Aesop wrote his famous **Fables**.

The fity-two cards in a normal pack are meant to symbolize the number of weeks in a year.

Americans drink over three billion pints of water a year.

SEPTEMBER 11

The radical English writer D.H. Lawrence was born on this day in 1885. He suffered a bad attack of bronchitis when only two weeks old, and was ill for the rest of his life. In 1902 he went down with pneumonia, and fourteen years later, at the age of thirty-one, he developed tuberculosis, the disease which finally killed him in 1930. Ironically, his final words were: 'I am getting better.'

The prison on the Isle of Sark has room for only two people.

Gorillas can't swim.

Battersea Dogs' Home has to deal with about 15,000 stray dogs every year.

Verdi's opera, 'Aida', was written to commemorate the opening of the Suez Canal.

SEPTEMBER 12

The first policewoman ever was appointed on 12 September 1910 in America. She was Alice Wells of the Los Angeles Police Department.

Cubans believe that it is dangerous to walk in the moonlight with a bare head.

Sunglasses were originally worn by Hollywood film stars not to look 'cool', but to protect their eyes against the harsh studio lights.

The teeth of a snail are situated along the length of its tongue.

SEPTEMBER (13)

The French film actress, Claudette Colbert, was born on 13 September 1905. She won an Academy Award for her role opposite Clark Gable in the 1934 film 'It Happened One Night'. It was the first movie to win all four major awards — Best Actor, Best Actress, Best Director, and Best Film — a distinction it shares with only one other film, 'One Flew Over The Cuckoo's Nest'.

King Constantine of Greece won an Olympic gold medal for sailing.

The Ethiopian Church regards Pontius Pilate as a saintly man.

Boxwood sinks in water.

Horses clean themselves by rolling around in the dust.

SEPTEMBER (14)

The Duke of Wellington died on this day in 1852. At his funeral in St Paul's Cathedral, there were seven thousand gas lamps placed all around the church to light up the procession.

In medical language, a moron is more intelligent than an idiot.

One tonne of uranium can produce the same amount of energy as 30,000 tonnes of coal.

Crickets hear things through their knees.

Submarines were invented in the early seventeenth century.

SEPTEMBER 15

Anton Von Webern, the German composer, died on 15 September 1945. After being banished from Germany at the start of World War Two by the Nazis, he spent the war in Austria, where, on this day in 1945, he was accidentally shot by an American army sentry after failing to answer a challenge to reveal his identity.

An ant can pull a load three hundred times its own weight.

Uranus was originally named 'georgium sidium' after George III of England.

America didn't have a national anthem until 1931.

The Ancient Chinese thought that sperm came from the brain.

SEPTEMBER 16

King Henry V of England was born on 16 September 1387. In 1414, at a time when Henry was considering whether he had a right to the throne of France, the Dauphin of France sent him a large sealed box as a present. It contained hundreds of tennis balls, and was meant to be a jibe at Henry for spending more time on the tennis court than on the battlefield. Henry got his revenge the following year, when England won the crucial Battle of Agincourt.

Albert Einstein failed his University Entrance exams at his first attempt.

In 1945, some starlings perched on the second hand of Big Ben in London, causing it to lose five minutes.

Your hair stands on end just before you are struck by lightning.

Three angels are mentioned by name in the bible — Gabriel, Michael, and Lucifer.

SEPTEMBER (17)

King James II of England died on 17 September 1685. He had some trouble during his reign with the Duke of Monmouth, who believed that he was the rightful heir to the Throne. In 1685, James had him executed, but as he was about to be buried, someone pointed out that the Duke had never had his portrait painted. His head was quickly sewn back onto his body, and the sitting began. The picture is now hanging in the National Portrait Gallery in London.

Napoléon travelled in a bullet-proof coach.

Alcohol doesn't warm the body up, but actually causes your body temperature to drop.

Fifty per cent of the world's population live in under five per cent of the total land area.

Water-lilies nearly three feet across grow in the Amazon Basin.

SEPTEMBER (18)

The film actress Greta Garbo, who was christened Greta Gustafsson, was born on 18 September 1905. She made her screen debut at the age of sixteen in an advertising film called 'How Not To Wear Clothes'.

The Chinese are very partial to a soup made from birds' nests.

Former US President, Jimmy Carter, is certain that he has seen a UFO.

The Queen is not allowed inside the House of Commons.

Heroin was originally thought to be a possible cure for opium addiction.

SEPTEMBER 19

On 19 September 1893, New Zealand became the first country in the world to give women the right to vote. The United States only followed suit some twenty-seven year later.

The Spanish often used urine to clean their teeth.

The right side of the human brain controls the left side of the body and vice versa.

Gorillas do not eat meat.

Ninety per cent of all fires are man-made.

SEPTEMBER 20

Jacob Grimm died on this day in 1863. He is most famous for the book of fairy tales he collected with his brother Wilhelm, but he was also a great linguist and inaugurated the important German Dictionary in 1852. It was finally completed by other scholars in 1960.

Canada's coastline is six times longer than that of Australia.

There are no bones in an elephant's trunk, just 40,000 muscles.

'Bulimia' is the name given to a disease where the sufferer will eat for up to fifteen hours at one stretch.

Cows' milk contains much more protein than human milk.

SEPTEMBER (21)

The novelist, Sir Walter Scott, died on 21 September 1832. The story of Walter Raleigh gallantly placing his cloak across a puddle for Queen Elizabeth, though originated by the historian Thomas Fuller, was very much kept alive by Scott in his popular romance, **Kenilworth**. In Scott's version the Queen asks Raleigh never to clean his cloak again, but to preserve it as a symbol of his gallantry.

The peacock is the symbol of resurrection in many pieces of early Christian art.

A normal spider has about six hundred silk glands on its body which it uses to spin its web.

The Italians used to block the tops of their wine bottles with oil before they thought of using cork.

The British airship, **R101**, which crashed on its maiden flight in 1930, cost £2 million to build.

SEPTEMBER (22)

On 22 September 1955, Britain's first commercial television channel began broadcasting. The first product to be advertised was Gibbs SR toothpaste.

During the Middle Ages, nearly a third of every year was given over to religious holidays.

Bikinis were named after the Bikini Atoll in the Pacific, where the Americans carried out a series of atomic bomb tests.

The River Thames froze over in the winter of 1890-91.

In 1933, the Royal Mint only produced four pennies.

SEPTEMBER (23)

The actor, Mickey Rooney, was born today in 1922 with the original name of Joe Yule Junior. Though only five feet three inches tall, he has obviously been a hit with the opposite sex all his life, marrying a grand total of seven times (so far!). His need to keep up his multiple alimony payments was undoubtedly a major cause of his bankruptcy in 1962.

Scotland exports sand to Saudi Arabia.

Big Ben in London is not the name of the clock, but the bell inside it.

Cats spend well over half of their lives asleep.

Our muscles cannot push, they can only pull.

SEPTEMBER (24)

The American writer, F. Scott Fitzgerald, was born on 24 September 1896. For most of his life he suffered from an oversecretion of insulin which resulted in an abnormally low blood-sugar level. To compensate for this, Fitzgerald used to drink heavily-sweetened coffee, and he had a craving for Coca-Cola and fudge. More seriously, this condition made him crave hugh quantities of alcohol, and he was certainly a heavy drinker for much of his life.

The 'white' statues of Ancient Rome and Greece were originally painted in bright colours.

Cucumbers are fruits, not vegetables.

The average-sized man would need a six-foot-long breastbone to be able to fly like a bird.

During the sixteenth century, you could not leave Japan without official permission.

SEPTEMBER (25)

On 25 September 1978, Mary Fuller was driving along a road in San Diego, California, when a human body came crashing through her car windscreen. It had been thrown clear of a plane crash nearby.

The Chenchu tribe in India believe that if you conceive a child at night it will be born blind.

The dog, Rin Tin Tin, was voted the most popular film performer of the year in 1926.

One of the most efficient ways of cleaning your teeth is to chew on a stick.

Horses can sleep standing up.

SEPTEMBER (26)

The American-born poet, T.S. Eliot, was born on 26 September 1888. I wonder if anyone ever pointed out to him that his name read backwards almost spells 'toilets'.

There is a red star called Epsilon Aurigae which is 27,000 million times bigger than our Sun.

The Americans had already sent an invitation to the opening of the Panama Canal to the Swiss navy, before they realized their mistake.

Some British zoos have had to put their lionesses on the pill to prevent unwanted pregnancies.

In Medieval England, the blacksmith used to re-set dislocated bones.

SEPTEMBER (27)

The film actress, Clara Bow, died on 27 September 1965. In 1921 she won a national fame and fortune contest for which the first prize was a role in a motion picture, and soon she became one of the leading silent stars of her age. Her sexual appetite was legendary, and there is even a story about her once 'entertaining' the entire University of Southern California football team.

The American composer, George Gershwin, suffered from chronic constipation for most of his adult life.

Canada has more lakes than the rest of the world put together.

Howard Hughes, the eccentric millionaire, originated the cantilever bra.

Though Switzerland is a neutral country, it has compulsory military service.

SEPTEMBER (28)

On 28 September 1894, Marks and Spencer opened their first shop — a penny bazaar in Manchester. They have, of course, expanded since then, and now over sixty per cent of the women in Britain buy their underwear from their shops all over the country.

No females are allowed on the peninsula of Mount Athos in Greece.

Charles Blondin once cooked an omelette while standing on his tightrope over the Niagara Falls.

White ants are not ants; they are termites.

The manufacturers of 'Monopoly' print more 'money' each year than the United States Treasury.

SEPTEMBER 29

The Liverpool Football Club Manager, Bill Shankly, died on this day in 1981. His dedication to football was total, and when he was once asked whether football was a matter of life and death to him, he replied: 'No — it's more important than that.'

Admiral Nelson never fully got over his seasickness.

The female ants are the ones who do all the work.

The Soma plant is thought to be sacred in India, and has over one hundred hymns dedicated to it.

Even fairly well-educated people use only one per cent of the possible words in the English language when talking to each other.

SEPTEMBER 30

The legendary film actor, James Dean, died on this day in 1955. If he had lived to see 1984, he would be fifty-three years old.

Gale warnings were first issued in 1861.

Johann Sebastian Bach wrote an operetta about coffee.

It is estimated that there are nearly half a million sauna baths in Finland.

The last time British troops fought in scarlet uniforms was during the Ashanti Campaign.

OCTOBER

The famous Egyptian Sphinx was carved out of a single piece of stone.

General Eisenhower, born on 14 October 1890, and I met only once, and not under the best of circumstances.

I was doing my National Service in Germany when an order came through that Ike was going to pay us a visit. My platoon was told to start digging fox-holes for him to inspect. The trouble was it started raining before he arrived and the fox-holes became crotch-deep in water. We'd been standing in them for hours by the time he finally showed up.

I don't know why he chose to speak to me, but when he looked down at me and asked encouragingly if I was thinking of staying on in the army, I answered like a true Cockney and said I wasn't. That got me confined to barracks for a month.

OCTOBER (1)

The English actress, Julie Andrews, was born on
1 October 1935. After the phenomenal success of 'The
Sound of Music' and 'Mary Poppins', she became
typecast as the sweet English rose, and in 1966 she
was quoted as saying: 'I don't want to be thought of
as wholesome.'

Honey-bees die after they deliver their first sting.

The famous Egyptian Sphinx was carved out of a
single piece of stone.

A real diamond should be cold to the touch.

Madame de la Bresse left a large amount of money
in her will to provide clothes for snowmen.

OCTOBER (2)

The writer, Graham Greene, was born on 2 October
1904. Most of his novels revolve around the
connection between Catholicism and modern life,
yet Greene himself was originally an Anglican, and
only converted to the Roman Catholic Religion.

Though the normal year has 365 days, the lunar
year has only 364.

White bread was originally used only in church
services.

There is a waterfall in Hawaii which goes up rather
than down.

The French call the Battle of Waterloo, the Battle of
Mont St Jean.

OCTOBER (3)

As long ago as 3 October 1811, a county cricket match was played between the women of Hampshire and the women of Surrey.

Atilla the Hun died on his wedding night.

All the continents of the world are thinner in the south than in the north — except Antarctica.

There is a city in the Sahara which is built entirely of salt.

There is only one lake in Scotland, the other areas of inland water are called lochs.

OCTOBER (4)

The American rock singer, Janis Joplin, died on 4 October 1970. She left $2,500 in her will 'so that my friends can get blasted after I'm gone.'

A starfish can turn its stomach inside out.

A Japanese sergeant hid in the jungles of Guam, and only surrendered twenty-eight years after the end of World War Two.

What we call a 'black eye' is called a 'blue eye' in Germany.

Sea-otters have two coats of fur.

172

OCTOBER 5

The English champion jockey, Gordon Richards, rode his twelfth consecutive winner in three days on 5 October 1933. He rode eleven of them at Chepstow Racecourse, following the initial winner at Nottingham.

Ships can travel faster in cold water than in warm.

Eggs are sold on bits of string in Korea.

At the start of this century, there was an outbreak of the plague in Sussex.

The Ancient Romans used to toast a woman's health by drinking a glass of wine for every letter of her name.

OCTOBER 6

On 6 October 1850, Alfred, Lord Tennyson died. Both Tennyson and his predecessor, William Wordsworth, wore exactly the same suit to the ceremony which marked their inauguration as Poet Laureate. And both borrowed it off another man, Samuel Rogers.

It is still possible under English law to prosecute fortune-tellers.

Henry Morgan, an infamous pirate, later became Lieutenant-Governor of Jamaica.

The duck-billed platypus is the only animal which has poisonous glands.

The largest meat-eating land animal in Britain is the badger.

OCTOBER 7

The American who invented a revolutionary process for deep-freezing food died on 7 October 1956. His name was Clarence Birdseye.

Cars were first started with ignition keys in 1949.

In Korea everyone flies a kite during the first week of a new year. The kites are then released to carry away all their bad luck.

The first gramophone record consisted of only five words — 'Mary had a little lamb.'

If you have a fear of beds, you are suffering from clinophobia.

OCTOBER 8

On 8 October 1976, a light aeroplane flew over the Piazza Venezia in Rome and dropped hundreds of bank notes onto the heads of unsuspecting passersby. The mysterious pilot was never found.

Hummingbirds can't walk.

The practice of numbering houses only began in London in 1764.

A normal swarm of locusts would consist of at least one million insects.

The writer, Rudyard Kipling, only ever used black ink.

OCTOBER 9

The singer-songwriter, John Lennon, was born on 9 October 1940 during an air raid. He was given the patriotic middle name of Winston.

Moths have neither mouths nor stomachs.

The Marquis de Pelier was put in prison for fifty years after he dared to whistle at Marie-Antoinette.

Pope Bendict IX was elected to office at the age of eleven.

The cashew-nut belongs to the same family as poison ivy.

OCTOBER 10

The Italian composer, Giuseppe Verdi, was born on 10 October 1813. His operas were hugely successful during his lifetime, and many contained a powerful political message. A popular joke at the time was that the initials of his name stood for 'Viva Emmanuelle Re d'Italia' (long live King Emmanuelle of Italy).

The poet, John Keats, worked as a dresser at Guy's Hospital in London.

The first woman to take a seat in the British House of Commons, Lady Astor, was born in America.

A group of geese on the ground is called a gaggle, but becomes a skein when airborne.

Solar energy was used as a source of power in the seventeenth century.

OCTOBER (11)

The food manufacturer, H.J. Heinz, was born today in 1844. He will go down in history as the 'inventor' of baked beans, well over eight million tins of which are sold each year.

Lobsters have blue blood.

William Shakespeare was the first person to use the word 'lonely'.

In spite of its hump, the backbone of a camel is perfectly straight.

Members of the Ibo tribe in Nigeria paint half their bodies white and half black to indicate that they are half body and half spirit.

OCTOBER (12)

An ordinary English nurse called Edith Cavell helped over two hundred Allied soldiers to escape from German-occupied Belgium during World War One. She was executed by firing squad on 12 October 1915.

The game of table-tennis was originally called 'gossamer'.

Dogs' teeth were used as a form of currency in the Solomon Islands until recently.

The glass cat-fish is almost totally transparent.

Richard Wagner composed some of his music while wearing fancy dress.

OCTOBER (13)

On 13 October 1892, there was a Parliamentary by-election at Cirencester in Gloucestershire. Both the Liberal and the Conservative candidates polled exactly the same number of votes, and there was no alternative but to order a new election.

There are over three times as many countries north of the equator as there are south of it.

Queen Ranavalona of Madagascar decreed that if any of her subjects appeared in her dreams, they would be killed.

A pound of lemons contains more sugar than a pound of strawberries.

There were no actresses at the time of William Shakespeare.

OCTOBER (14)

Dwight D. Eisenhower was born on 14 October 1890. He grew up to become the first five-star general in American history, and in 1944 he helped plan the Allied invasion of Europe. The parents of this great military figure were members of a fundamentalist religious organization called the River Brethren Sect, which openly advocates pacifism.

During the seventeenth century, the German State of Munster formally exiled a plague of fleas for a period of ten years.

None of Socrates' writings actually survive.

The famous conductor, Stokowski, conducted his first orchestra at the age of twelve.

Red Indians used to smoke through their noses.

OCTOBER (15)

The Roman poet, Virgil, was born on this day in 70 BC. He is meant to have possessed a bath that could cure anything, and on one occasion he held a lavish funeral for his favourite pet fly.

The largest eggs in the world are laid by sharks.

The Western hero, Buffalo Bill, didn't hunt buffalo, he hunted bison.

The oldest museum in the world is the Ashmolean in Oxford.

Under one per cent of the islands in the Caribbean are inhabited.

OCTOBER (16)

Oscar Wilde, the Irish writer of many talents, was born in Dublin on 16 October 1854. He became famous for his quick wit, and on his first visit to America was asked by the Customs officials whether he had anything to declare. 'I have nothing to declare except my genius,' quipped Wilde.

The Persian Emperor, Cyrus the Great, once sentenced a river to death because his favourite horse had drowned in it.

Bombay duck is made from dried fish.

Windsor Castle, the country residence of the British Royal Family, is the largest castle in the world that is still inhabited.

Nine-tenths of the Vitamin C present in Brussels Sprouts is lost when they are cooked.

OCTOBER (17)

The American stunt-rider, Evel Knievel, was born on 17 October 1938. He has become known for his daredevil motorbike jumps across ever-widening chasms. He has broken over 100 bones in his lifetime, and now claims that he is so used to being operated on that he doesn't even need a proper anaesthetic.

Once they have been picked, oranges cease to ripen.

Humans shed one complete layer of skin every four weeks.

Christopher Columbus' crew on his voyage to the New World consisted of about one hundred convicts.

Venus is the only planet in our Solar System which rotates in a clockwise direction.

OCTOBER (18)

It is tempting to think that this day has some sort of religious significance, because one Pope was born and two others died on 18 October. Pope Pius II was born in 1405, Pope Gregory XII died in 1417, and finally Pope Pius III died in 1503.

The word 'amen' is used not only by Christians, but by Jews and Moslems as well.

There is a reference to baseball in Jane Austen's novel, **Northanger Abbey**.

The most common first name in the world is Mohammed.

The Arabian Gulf States of Qatar, Bahrain, and Kuwait — three of the richest countries in the world — do not charge income tax.

OCTOBER 19

The 'King of Bells' in the Kremlin was cast on 19 October 1773. It is over twenty feet high and weighs nearly two hundred tons, but it has never been rung as it cracked on being released from the mould.

The US Air Force consisted of only fifty men at the outbreak of the First World War.

Criminals were branded in China until the turn of the century.

The Great Pyramid at Cheops could be called the largest sundial in the world.

An Englishman called Henry Lewis was able to play billiards with his nose.

OCTOBER 20

Sir Richard Burton, who died on 20 October 1890, was one of the most accomplished men of his generation. He was both a man of action — a swordsman and explorer — and an intellectual. Not only did he write forty-three travel books and two volumes of poetry, but he also translated sixteen volumes of the **Arabian Nights**, two volumes of Latin poetry, six volumes of Portugese literature, as well as books in Hindustani, Arabic, and Sanskrit. In all, he spoke twenty languages.

The English swallow takes about thirty days to migrate to Africa.

More perfume is used in Russia than in any other country in the world.

Silkworms are not worms, but caterpillars.

You cannot transmit a radio signal from a submerged submarine to land.

OCTOBER (21)

On 21 October 1966, disaster struck the small Welsh mining village of Aberfan, when a colliery slag tip slid down the side of a hill and engulfed a row of houses, a farm, and a school. Of the 144 people who died, 116 were children.

Mozart's opera, 'Don Giovanni', was performed in public the day after it was written.

Jack the Ripper was left-handed.

The binoculars which are widely available today are more powerful than Galileo's telescope.

The model of an ape used for the 1933 film 'King Kong', was only eighteen inches tall.

OCTOBER (22)

On 22 October 1797, the first parachute jump in history was made over Parc Monceau in Paris by André Garnerin. He did not jump from an aeroplane, though, but a balloon.

Every day, seven-and-a-half million tons of water evaporate from the Dead Sea.

More people are killed each year by bees than by poisonous snakes.

You **can** mix oil and water — simply add a little soap.

Poodles don't moult.

OCTOBER (23)

The Battle of El Alamein began on 23 October 1942. Fewer British soldiers died in this week-long battle than died in the Battle of Oudenarde in 1708, which lasted just one day.

Cervantes, the Spanish author who wrote **Don Quixote**, had only one arm.

There is a bird-eating spider in South America which has a leg-span of ten inches.

If you lived on the planet Mercury, you would have four birthdays in a single Earth year.

John Wayne's real name was Marion Morrison.

OCTOBER (24)

The Norwegian diplomat, Vidkun Quisling, was born on 24 October 1887. During the Second World War, he became a Nazi collaborator, and was executed by firing squad in 1945. His name has gone down in history as the one given to all traitors.

There is a type of cow called a 'Why'.

Japanese cherry trees do not bear any fruit — they are grown purely for decoration.

The members of All Soul's College, Oxford are not called students, they are called fellows.

April Fool's Day is referred to as Boob Day in Spain.

OCTOBER (25)

Two of the most famous battles in British history were fought on this day. In 1415, Henry V scored his famous victory at Agincourt, wiping out 1,500 French cavalry in the process. In 1854, at Balaclava, the suicidal Charge of the Light Brigade was begun by Lord Cardigan. In the space of twenty minutes, nearly 250 men and over 500 horses were slaughtered.

The common house-fly can transmit thirty different diseases to man.

The dormouse was considered a delicacy in Ancient Rome.

The British Army were doing the 'goose step' long before the Nazis made it famous.

The most common name for a public house in Britain is 'The Red Lion'.

OCTOBER (26)

The late Shah of Iran was born on 26 October 1919. He once lost one and a half million dollars playing Poker, after which he decided to give it up in favour of Bridge.

The Siberian larch accounts for one-fifth of the world's trees.

The stripes of a zebra are white, not black.

In America, a man called Al Cohol was once charged with being drunk.

Shooting-stars are not stars, but burning meteors.

OCTOBER (27)

The Welsh poet Dylan Thomas, was born on this day in 1914. He is most famous for his poetry, but he also wrote a very popular radio play called 'Under Milk Wood'. The action is set in a fictional Welsh village called 'Llareggub', which spells 'Buggerall' backwards.

Only human beings sleep on their backs.

The Red Sea is not red, it's blue.

Doris Day began her career as a dancer, and only became a singer after she broke her leg.

Lord Palmerston's last words were: 'Die, my dear doctor? Why, that's the last thing I shall do.'

OCTOBER (28)

The Statue of Liberty was officially dedicated on 28 October 1886. It was a present from the French Government to mark the one-hundredth anniversary of the Declaration of Independence, and was designed by Gustave Eiffel.

Pepsi-Cola was originally designed as a hangover cure.

There is a river called 'Aa' in France.

More people live in Asia than all the other continents put together.

Light from the Sun takes about eight-and-a-half minutes to reach the Earth.

OCTOBER (29)

Sir Walter Raleigh was executed on 29 October 1618. It is widely thought that he introduced tobacco to Europe, but the distinction should be accorded to someone else — a Frenchman called Jean Nicot.

There are over two thousand crown princes in Arabia.

It is bad luck for an Australian Aborigine to speak to his mother-in-law.

To type the word 'typewriter', you only have to use the top row of letter keys.

Midges beat their tiny wings about one thousand times a second.

OCTOBER (30)

On 30 October 1938, Orson Welles did a radio version of H.G. Wells' **The War of The Worlds**. The programme, which dealt with a fictional Martian invasion of the world, caused panic throughout America despite constant assurances that it was not real 'news'.

Lord Byron's last word was: 'Goodnight.'

Duelling is legal in Uruguay, providing both participants are blood donors.

The average iceburg weighs twenty million tons.

Only nine nations competed at the first modern Olympics, held in Athens in 1896.

OCTOBER (31)

The famous escapologist, Harry Houdini, died on this day in 1926. For a man who performed so many outrageous stunts, it is ironic that he should have been killed by a simple blow to the stomach, delivered when the great man was unprepared.

There is a bye-law in New York which forbids women to smoke in the street.

Wilfred Baddely won the men's singles title at Wimbledon at the age of nineteen.

Goethe wrote a story in seven different languages when he was ten.

The first breakfast cereal to be produced was 'Shredded Wheat'.

NOVEMBER

French painter, Paul Gauguin, helped in the construction of the Panama Canal.

The Portuguese capital, Lisbon, was hit by a particularly bad earthquake on 1 November 1755. That was just one of many disasters to strike it. Two hundred and twelve years later, over four hundred people were drowned in horrific floods.

We filmed 'A Hill in Korea' on the slopes of Monte Junto there in 1956. We used to leave Lisbon every morning in bright sunshine but by the time we arrived on the set, it was bucketing down – and this was a regular occurrence.

During one downpour I asked one of the locals what Monte Junto meant. He told me the mountain was known by another name locally, the 'Monte de Nuevo', which means 'Mountain of Mist'. because it's always covered with cloud. We seemed to have picked the one mountain in Portugal where you could guarantee rain!

NOVEMBER (1)

On this day in 1755, Lisbon in Portugal suffered one of the most powerful earthquakes the world has ever seen. Although it happened over two hundred years ago, before machines had been invented to measure such phenomena, experts believe it may have had a magnitude of as much as 9. The biggest measured earthquake in modern times had a magnitude of 8.9.

Sir Laurence Olivier is a member of the Hilda Ogden Appreciation Society.

The French painter, Paul Gauguin, helped in the construction of the Panama Canal.

More people in the world drink goats' milk than cows' milk.

NOVEMBER (2)

Today, in 1924, the first crossword appeared in Britain. It was published in the **Sunday Express**.

All sweet things are tasted at the tip of the tongue only.

George Bernard Shaw was a vegetarian.

A rat can last longer without water than a camel.

Karl Marx worked as a political columnist for the **New York Tribune**.

NOVEMBER 3

On 3 November 1903, the small country of Panama became independent. The Panama hat, apparently one of its most famous exports, does, in fact, originate from Ecuador.

Late in her life, Queen Elizabeth I became totally bald.

A mole can dig a tunnel over 250 feet long in just one night.

One of the original ingredients in Coca-Cola was the drug cocaine.

The real title of the famous painting known as the 'Mona Lisa', is 'La Giaconda'.

NOVEMBER 4

On this day in 1963, The Beatles played at the Royal Variety Performance in front of the Queen Mother and assorted dignitaries. Introducing a song, John Lennon, famous for his cynical wit, quipped: 'Those in the cheaper seats clap. The rest of you, rattle your jewellery.'

The animal with the biggest brain in relation to its body is the ant.

Peanuts are used in the production of dynamite.

Babies under six months old can breathe and swallow at the same time — we can't.

The kilt originated, not in Scotland, but in France.

NOVEMBER (5)

The fifth of November is celebrated as Guy Fawkes' Day, in remembrance of an unsuccessful attempt to blow up the Houses of Parliament in 1605. During the eighteenth century it was actually illegal **not** to celebrate this day. The law was eventually repealed in 1859.

The bat is the only mammal that can fly.

One of the most famous statues in the world, 'The Thinker', by Rodin, is actually a portrait of the Italian poet, Dante.

The Ancient Chinese used to organize fights between crickets, sometimes even weighing the insects as they do in modern boxing.

Sneezes can sometimes travel as fast as one hundred miles an hour.

NOVEMBER (6)

On this day in 1922, Howard Carter discovered the amazing treasures of Tutankhamen's tomb. Unfortunately, the sponsor of the exploration, Lord Carnarvon, died five months later, and so was never able to view the full splendours of the inner tomb. Some people still believe he died of the 'Pharaoh's curse'.

Lord Byron, one of the most sought-after men of his age, had a club foot.

Scientists insist that everybody dreams — it's just that some people don't remember their dreams.

The most under-used letter in the English language is the letter 'Q'.

Crocodiles cannot move their tongues because they are firmly attached to the roof of their mouths.

NOVEMBER (7)

The Evangelist, Billy Graham, was born today in 1918. Nicknamed 'The Preaching Windmill', he once claimed that Heaven is exactly 1,600 miles above the Earth.

Sharks are totally immune to cancer.

The human brain is about eighty per cent water.

There are over thirty thousand separate verses in The Bible.

The Greek playwright, Aeschylus, is thought to have been killed when an eagle dropped a tortoise on his head.

NOVEMBER (8)

The man who wrote the horror classic **Dracula**, Bram Stoker, was born today in 1847. Though many people would decry the suggestion that vampires exist, it was a part of English Law until 1824 to drive a wooden stake through the heart of any suicide victim to prevent them from turning into a vampire.

There are over one hundred different species of butterfly.

Nothing can be burned twice.

Ninety-seven per cent of the world's water is to be found in the oceans.

There are something like twenty words in the Eskimo language which describe different kinds of snow.

NOVEMBER (9)

American actress, Katherine Hepburn, was born today in 1909. Her success record at the annual Academy Awards is phenomenal. She has been nominated thirteen times, and has won the Oscar for Best Actress four times.

Tobacco may be bad for your health when smoked, but it has some nutritional value if eaten.

The French phrase for a 'French kiss' is an 'English kiss'.

The Sahara Desert is about the same size as the whole of Europe.

In relation to their size, grasshoppers have the greatest jumping ability of any animal.

NOVEMBER (10)

The late actor Richard Burton came into the world today in 1925. Undoubtedly a great actor, he was perhaps most famous for his stormy relationship with Elizabeth Taylor. He showered her with presents during their two marriages, including a £500,000 diamond and a £60,000 mink coat.

The world is not totally round. In fact, it bulges in the middle and is flatter at both ends.

Hindu women dye their teeth red to make themselves more attractive.

Cows have four stomachs.

The modern bra came about after women athletes at the 1928 Olympics complained that such competitive running often resulted in severe bruising.

NOVEMBER (11)

American soldier, General Patton, was born on 11 November 1885. He believed that he had had six previous lives, including a spell in the army of Alexander the Great, and a period as a prehistoric warrior.

Caterpillars have over two thousand muscles in their bodies.

The colour of mourning at funerals in Turkey is violet.

The brain takes up a quarter of all the oxygen used by the human body.

The shortest verse in The Bible is 'Jesus wept'.

NOVEMBER (12)

On this day in 1956, the largest iceberg in the world was discovered in the South Pacific Ocean. It was bigger than Belgium.

Roman children used to wear miniature phalluses around their necks to protect them from evil.

More herrings are eaten worldwide than any other fish.

Every thoroughbred racehorse that exists in the world today, can be traced back to the three Arabian stallions which arrived in England in the 1700s.

George Washington often carried a sundial around with him to tell the time, rather than a watch.

NOT MANY PEOPLE KNOW THAT

NOVEMBER 13

The writer, R.L. Stevenson, was born today in 1850. He claimed that his famous story, **The Strange Case of Dr Jekyll and Mr Hyde**, appeared to him in its totality in a dream one night.

Henry Ford is said to have kept the inventor Edison's dying breath sealed in a bottle.

Only female bees do any work for the hive.

Cleopatra married her brother Ptolemy.

The banana cannot reproduce itself without the help of man.

NOVEMBER 14

On 14 November 1973, Princess Anne and Captain Mark Phillips were married in London. At the Wolverhampton Races that day, the two-thirty 'Wedding Stakes' was won by a horse called 'Royal Mark'.

Some Chinese typewriters have over five thousand different characters.

Male monkeys can go bald just like their human counterparts.

In Flanders, there is an annual ceremony involving the swallowing of live fish.

Nero could not have fiddled while Rome burnt — violins were not invented until much later.

NOVEMBER (15)

The last of the Manchu Emperors, Pu Yi, came to power today in 1908, aged just two-and-a-half years. After the takeover of Mao Tse Tung and the Communist Party, he ended up as an odd-job-man at the Botanical Gardens in Peking.

During the Middle Ages, many animals were executed for crimes such as heresy and witchcraft.

Your nose continues to grow throughout your life.

Penguins have the ability to change salt water into fresh water.

The word 'love', which is used in tennis to mean 'no score', comes from the French word 'L'oeuf', which means 'egg'. An egg was presumably thought to be shaped like a zero.

NOVEMBER (16)

Probably the greatest meteor shower of all time occurred on this night in 1966, in the skies above the northern part of the Pacific Ocean. At one point more than two thousand meteors a minute passed overhead.

Everyone's tongue print is different.

Natural gas has no smell. An odour is added to prevent people ignoring dangerous gas leaks.

Marcel Proust wrote a lot of his work in bed.

The Greek National Anthem has 158 verses.

NOVEMBER (17)

On this day in 1913, the first ship sailed through the newly-completed Panama Canal. Amid the celebrations, there was also cause for great sorrow. Over twenty-five thousand lives were lost during the construction of the Canal.

The original name given to the butterfly was the 'flutterby'.

During the French Revolution, the Kings, Queens, and Jacks were removed from all card packs, because they were considered too royalist.

You breathe nearly two gallons of air a minute.

Only humans cry.

NOVEMBER (18)

The highest-paid pianist ever was born today back in 1860. Ignace Paderewski earned nearly two million pounds during his career, making two hundred thousand pounds in one performance in 1922. He later became the Prime Minister of Poland.

There are only two words in the English language which have all the vowels in the correct order — 'facetious' and 'abstemious'.

There are more Irish in New York than in the whole of Dublin.

Fifteen million blood cells are produced and destroyed every second.

The male praying mantis can continue copulating with the female even after she has started eating him.

NOVEMBER (19)

Abraham Lincoln made a famous speech on this day in 1863, after the crucial Battle of Gettysburg which was the turning point in the American Civil War. His oration finished with the now-legendary promise of 'Government of the people, by the people, for the people'.

The Olympics of AD 60 had an unusual competitor in Emperor Nero. Though he was a terrible athlete, he managed to win every event which he entered.

Robert the Bruce, the heroic Scottish King, was a leper.

In Iceland, the telephone directories list people according to their first names.

The Commissioner of Education on the Virgin Islands in 1980 was called A. Moron.

NOVEMBER (20)

Queen Elizabeth and Prince Philip married in Westminster Abbey on this day in 1947. Among their wedding presents were a racehorse from the Aga Khan, and a hand-made piece of lace from Mahatma Gandhi.

During the American Civil War, maggots were used to eat away the dead tissue around wounds.

The Duke of Wellington suggested that the Houses of Parliament be built on the banks of the River Thames, so that it could never be surrounded by an angry mob.

Chinese rulers used to use giant clams' shells as baths.

In 1457, James II of Scotland banned football and golf because they were distracting his men from the more important sport of archery, which he considered so crucial to the national defence.

NOVEMBER (21)

The skull of the ancient Piltdown man, said to be an invaluable link in the chain of human evolution, was discovered by Charles Dawson on this day in 1912. Even though many scientists enthused about it, the discovery was eventually declared a hoax, and caused one of the greatest scandals of the day.

The first air raid in history occurred on 21 August 1849, when bombs with pre-set fuses were dropped from hot-air balloons on to the city of Venice.

Eleanor of Aquitaine was married to both the King of France and the King of England.

Lionel Rothschild, the first Jewish MP to be elected, had to wait until eleven years after his election in 1847 to take his seat in the House, because he was not allowed to take the oath according to the Jewish faith.

NOVEMBER (22)

On 22 November 1963, millions of people all over the world witnessed the assassination of President John F. Kennedy. Amazingly, at the time, it was not a felony under US Federal Law to kill the President.

In terms of physical effort, a watch-repairer probably uses twice as much energy dressing in the morning than he does in his normal working hours.

You can hold an alligator's mouth shut with one hand.

Cardinal Mezzofanti managed to master one hundred and fourteen different languages during his lifetime, as well as seventy-two dialects.

Sir Thomas Malory, famous for his fifteenth-century Arthurian romance, **Le Morte d'Arthur**, which dealt largely with the noble ideas of chivalry and courtly love, went to prison eight times for crimes including rape and armed robbery.

NOVEMBER (23)

Harpo Marx, the frizzy-haired Marx Brother with the dirty raincoat, was born today in 1893. although he acted the mute on film, Harpo could, in fact, speak quite normally.

The only animal with four knees is the elephant.

The seaweed which you find in the Pacific Ocean can be as much as six hundred feet long.

At least one million people a year in Asia and Africa die after being bitten by the malarial mosquito.

The game of lacrosse was invented by the American Red Indians.

NOVEMBER (24)

Charles Darwin's **The Origin of Species**, one of the most important books in the history of mankind, was published today in 1859. The phrase, 'The survival of the fittest', which is central to the book's argument, was not thought up by Darwin, however, but was borrowed from another scientist, Herbert Spencer, who had coined it a few years earlier.

Indian ink comes from China.

Maurice Ravel, famous for his 'Bolero', once wrote a piano piece for a one-handed man.

A foxhound once produced twenty-three puppies in just one litter.

Only ten words make up twenty per cent of everything we say.

NOVEMBER (25)

'The Mousetrap' by Agatha Christie opened in London on 25 November 1952. It is still running today, and is the longest-running show in the world.

Croissants were originally conceived not in France, but in Austria.

The sea snake is a hundred times more venomous than any snake to be found on dry land.

The Romans introduced bagpipes to Britain.

Beethoven used to pour iced water over his head to stimulate his brain, and so give him the necessary inspiration to write music.

NOVEMBER (26)

Today in 1764, a 'great storm' raged over the whole of England. Terrible damage was caused, and over eight thousand people are thought to have lost their lives.

Dr Roget wrote his famous **Thesaurus** in his spare time. It took him nearly fifty years to complete.

The proportion of right-handed to left-handed people in the world is reckoned to be about five to one.

A giant octopus once sank a schooner weighing 150 tons.

Queen Elizabeth II is an Anglican in England, but a Presbyterian in Scotland.

NOVEMBER (27)

On 27 November 1582, William Shakespeare married Anne Hathaway. The great writer was only eighteen years of age at the time.

In High Wycombe every year, all the local dignitaries, including the mayor, are publically weighed to see if they have grown fat at the taxpayers' expense.

Isiah Sellers, a journalist, took the pen-name 'Mark Twain' before his much more famous contemporary, Samuel Clemens. Both men worked as river pilots on the Mississippi, where 'Mark Twain' was a familiar technical term.

Both Mussolini and Hitler suffered from venereal disease.

The most prescribed drug in the United Kingdom is Valium.

NOVEMBER (28)

The English poet, William Blake, was born today in 1757. He was a visionary, and claimed to have lengthy talks with famous people in history, including many of the prophets. In fact, his long-suffering wife used to complain that she rarely saw him, since he was often in Heaven.

Instant coffee is not that new a phenomenon. It has been around since the middle of the eighteenth century.

The Amazon River basin, with its prodigious plant life, provides the world with about forty per cent of its oxygen.

Butterfly fish become very attached to each other, and go around in pairs rather like married couples.

Blond beards grow faster than dark ones.

NOVEMBER (29)

Giacomo Puccini, the composer of 'La Boheme', died on this day in 1924. His wife was so jealous of other women that she used to put bromide in his coffee to reduce his sex drive.

A bear which weighs five hundred pounds can give birth to a cub weighing as little as ten ounces.

The first of the five senses to deteriorate as you grow older is the sense of smell.

Lead pencils are not made of lead at all, but graphite.

A common form of greeting in Egypt is 'How do you sweat?'

NOVEMBER (30)

Sir Winston Churchill was born today in 1874. One of the most popular British politicians ever, and the winner of the Nobel Prize for Literature in 1953, he was not always a success on life. In fact, he was bottom of the class for much of his time at Harrow, and only managed to get into the Sandhurst Military Academy on his third attempt.

Gorillas stick out their tongues when they get angry.

There are no turkeys in Turkey.

King Louis XIV apparently had only three baths in his entire life.

DECEMBER

Most astronauts grow an inch or two during their period in space.

December 1943, Christmas-time to be exact, marked my first speaking part on stage. The show was 'Cinderella', the theatre was the school hall in North Runcton, Norfolk, and at the age of ten I was playing Baron Fitznoodle, father of the Ugly Sisters. They were both older than me and I fell head over heels in love with one of them, the twelve-year-old. NOT MANY PEOPLE KNOW THAT !

DECEMBER 1

Woody Allen, the American film-maker and comedian, was born today in 1935. His Oscar-winning film, 'Annie Hall', contained numerous examples of the tragi-comic wit which has become Allen's trademark. It's easy to see why he describes himself as being 'at two with nature'.

An Englishman once paid £12,000 for a racing pigeon.

Most astronauts grow an inch or two during their period in space.

There is only one metal which is liquid (at room temperature) — mercury.

Two different alphabets are used in Yugoslavia.

DECEMBER 2

The Marquis de Sade, the man who gave his name to sadism, died on this day in 1814. His books are still officially banned in France.

More than half the babies born every day arrive before breakfast.

Russia's October Revolution took place in November.

The chaffinch cannot sing anything original, it can only imitate the songs of other birds.

The Prime Minister is eleventh in the official British order of precedence.

DECEMBER (3)

On 3 December 1926, the famous mystery writer, Agatha Christie, disappeared after hearing of her husband's plan to continue his love affair with another woman. Ten days later she was found living in a health spa in Yorkshire. No explanation was given for her behaviour, though speculation ranged from amnesia to attempted suicide. The police-search for Agatha Christie was exhaustive, and was reputed to have included over fifteen thousand volunteers.

When two people meet in Tibet, they usually bump foreheads as a sign of greeting.

Piranha fish can strip a horse of all its flesh in under a minute.

There are about seven million lamp-posts in Britain.

Bagpipes can enter America tax-free.

DECEMBER (4)

On 4 December 1952, a freak weather change saw the City of London enveloped by a layer of deadly smog, which literally left people gasping for breath. After five days, the death toll came to over four thousand, and thousands more died later from related illnesses.

Elizabeth I had over eighty wigs to choose from.

At the first performance of Stravinsky's 'The Rite of Spring', there was a full-scale riot. The audience objected to what they regarded as the ballet's blatant obscenity.

Cuckoos lay their eggs in other birds' nests.

Chinese doctors used to prescribe marijuana for ailments such as malaria, gout, and absent-mindedness.

DECEMBER 5

Walt Disney, who was born today in 1901, went bankrupt early on in his life. His company, 'Laugh-O-Gram-Corp.', collapsed in 1923, but the young Walt soon recovered and went on to become one of the richest men in America.

On average, people are a quarter of an inch taller at night than they are during the day.

Charles I is the only English King ever to be beheaded.

There are about a thousand different words for 'camel' in Arabic.

The oldest fish on record is a sturgeon.

DECEMBER 6

On this day in 1957, the first American satellite was due to blast off into outer space amid world-wide Press interest. When the appointed time came, it only managed to get two feet off the ground, after which it promptly blew up.

The average life span in Ancient Rome was twenty-two years.

About one-sixth of the population of Britain eats custard at least once a day.

Though swifts can fly at speeds of up to one hundred miles an hour, their legs are so short that they are almost unable to walk.

Each day about ten million people celebrate the same birthday.

DECEMBER (7)

On 7 December 1858, Dr James Barry became Inspector-General of Hospitals in Queen Victoria's Army. Only after 'his' death in 1865, was it discovered that Dr Barry was in fact a woman. Apparently, she had originally joined the Army in pursuit of her lover who was an Army surgeon.

Probably the longest unbroken peace between major nations is that between England and Portugal. They have never been at war with each other.

George I of England could neither speak nor write English.

If you cut a starfish up into a sizeable chunks, each piece has the ability to grow into a whole new starfish.

Seventeen per cent of the world's caviar is consumed on the **QE2** every year.

DECEMBER (8)

One of history's eccentrics, Queen Christina of Sweden, was born today in 1626. She had a pathological fear of fleas, and had a small cannon built to kill the irritating insects. Its barrel measured about four inches, and it was specially designed to fire minute cannon-balls.

In Northern Europe, earrings were originally worn to stop evil spirits entering through people's ears.

It used to be considered unlucky to cut your nails on a Sunday.

Bulls can run faster uphill than downhill.

Over four hundred films have been made of the plays of William Shakespeare.

DECEMBER (9)

On this day in 1916, Issur Danielovitch Demsky was born. That was his real name — his stage name was Kirk Douglas.

There are over one hundred million light sensitive cells in the retina of the human eye.

A cat in Texas has had 420 kittens at the last count.

The poet Coleridge drank about half a gallon of laudanum a week at the height of his addiction.

The eastern slope of Mont Blanc is in Italy; the summit is in France.

DECEMBER (10)

Alfred Nobel died on 10 December 1896. The major invention of his life was dynamite, and although its importance was great, Nobel worried that he would go down in history as a propagator of violence and destruction. Thanks to a late change in his will, he is more likely to be remembered as the instigator of the world-famous Nobel Prizes.

Over fifty thousand pigeons were used as carrier birds in the Second World War.

Tarantulas can live for over two-and-a-half years without food.

No new buildings have been built in Dubrovnik since the eighteenth century.

In every country in the world, the life span of women is appreciably longer than that of men.

DECEMBER 11

Edward VIII, Duke of Windsor, announced his abdication at 10 pm on this day in 1936. He is the only English King never to be crowned.

Seals can dive to depths of one thousand feet.

The scientific term for fear of beards is pogonophobia.

A chimpanzee fooled the art world when his paintings were not only displayed in galleries and bought by collectors, but became the subject of learned critical argument.

A firm in Britain will sell you a fall-out shelter for the protection of the family pets.

DECEMBER 12

The inventor of the hovercraft, Sir Christopher Cockerell, finally got his idea patented on 12 December 1955. The first hovercraft public service came into being some six years later, when a twenty-four-passenger vehicle ran across the River Dee in England.

The music hall entertainer, Nosmo King, literally discovered his stage name while looking at a 'No Smoking' sign.

It is an offence to slam a car door in Switzerland.

No rain has ever been recorded in the Atacama desert in Chile.

King Charles VIII of France had six toes on one of his feet.

DECEMBER 13

Samuel Johnson, the man who wrote the first important English dictionary, died today in 1784. Though he suffered from a severe skin disease for most of his life, he was a prolific writer and a great wit. He once said to his biographer, Boswell, 'It matters not how a man dies, but how he lives'.

Six natives of Tanzania once drank insecticide in the hope that it would cure them of worms, insecticide being a killer of insects. All six died.

Rabbits sometimes eat their own faeces.

The Channel between England and France widens by about a foot every year.

Centipedes will eat meat.

DECEMBER 14

King George VI was born today in 1895. His Christian name was in fact Albert, but he rejected it in favour of George to respect Queen Victoria's wish that no future British King should bear her husband's name.

One hundred thousand small toads once fell out of the air and landed on a village in France.

Pigeons were the main source of fresh meat for the people of the Middle Ages.

The average modern jet uses about seventy thousand pounds of oxygen travelling from Europe to America.

There are something like 100,000 cats on the payroll of the British Civil Service.

DECEMBER (15)

Sitting Bull, the Red Indian Chief of the Sioux tribes, died on this day in 1890. His bones were originally laid to rest in North Dakota, but businessmen from his native South Dakota wanted to have him moved to a more natural resting place. When their campaign was rejected, they stole the bones, and they now reside in Sitting Bull Park, South Dakota.

Penguins can leap over six feet into the air.

During the Napoleonic Wars, a monkey was hanged for being a French spy.

The actress, Sarah Bernhardt, played the part of the teenage Juliet in Shakespeare's 'Romeo and Juliet' when she was seventy years old.

The world at the moment is in the middle of an ice age.

DECEMBER (16)

The great classical composer, Ludwig van Beethoven, was born on 16 December 1770. He was obsessed with music to the exclusion of almost everything else, and used to dress very scruffily. Indeed, his disregard for the dress conventions of his day led the authorities to arrest him on one occasion for the crime of vagrancy.

Karate, often regarded as Japan's national sport, did not come to that country until 1916.

Barnacles stay fastened to the same object for the whole of their lives.

Lightning strikes the earth about a hundred times every second.

The mullet fish only turns totally red after its death.

DECEMBER (17)

The Wright brothers launched the first sustained power-driven flight by an aeroplane on this day in 1903. The distance covered by their historic flying machine was less than the length of the modern Jumbo Jet.

Custer was the youngest general ever in the US Army. He was promoted at the age of twenty-three.

No two snowflakes have yet been discovered with the same crystal pattern.

Because of its gravitational pull, you weigh slightly less when the moon is directly overhead.

DECEMBER (18)

On 18 December 1865, slavery was finally abolished in the United States. On the same day in 1917, the US Congress submitted prohibition legislation to the states.

Clouds settle at a greater height during the day than they do at night.

Snails only mate once in their entire life, but it can take up to twelve hours for them to complete.

On average, one lead pencil can draw a line thirty-five miles long.

Tomatoes used to be called 'love apples'.

DECEMBER (19)

The English painter, Joseph Turner, died on this day in 1851. He was something of a prodigy as a child, and his father, who was a barber, used to sell his twelve-year-old son's drawings to amazed customers.

Cats were considered sacred animals in Ancient Egypt, and when they died, people used to shave off their eyebrows as a mark of respect.

Some of the singing parts in Handel's operas are specially written for men who have been castrated. Though popular in his own day, they are not (perhaps understandably) performed much nowadays.

Every time you step forward, you use fifty-four muscles.

Dogs are colour-blind.

DECEMBER (20)

Uri Geller, the professional psychic whose metal-bending powers shocked many scientists all over the world, was born on 20 December 1946. As to the origin of his alleged powers, Mr Geller maintains that they come from the distant planet of Hoova.

The tallest member of Parliament in Britain was six feet six inches tall.

Coffins which are due for cremation are usually made with plastic handles.

The orang-utan's warning signal to would-be aggressors is a loud belch.

DECEMBER (21)

The Tory Prime Minister, Benjamin Disraeli, was born today in 1804. He was noted for his oratory, and had a number of memorable exchanges in the House with his great rival William Gladstone. Asked what the difference between a calamity and a misfortune was, Disraeli replied, 'If Gladstone fell into the Thames it would be a misfortune, but if someone pulled him out again, it would be a calamity.'

On average, elephants sleep for about two hours a day.

The authorities do not allow tourists to take pictures of the Pygmies in Zambia.

Before the Second World War, it was considered a sacrilege even to touch an Emperor of Japan.

Australian termites have been known to build mounds twenty feet high, and at least one hundred feet wide.

DECEMBER (22)

Giacomo Puccini was born on 22 December 1858. He composed many famous operas such as 'La Bohème' and 'Madam Butterfly', but one of his lesser-known works is actually set in the Wild West at the time of the California Gold Rush. Its title is 'La Fanciulla del West', which loosely translated means 'The Girl of the Golden West'.

In relation to its size, the ordinary house spider is as much as eight times faster than an Olympic sprinter.

The largest muscle in the human body is the buttock muscle.

On a clear night, over two thousand stars are visible to the naked eye.

It costs more to send someone to a reform school than it does to send them to Eton.

DECEMBER (23)

The French critic, Saint-Beuve, was born on this day in 1804. On one occasion in his life he was unfortunate enough to get involved in a duel. When asked to choose his weapons, he replied, 'I choose spelling. You're dead.'

The richest ten per cent of the French people are approximately fifty times better off than the poorest ten per cent.

The juke-box derives its name from the old English word for dancing — to 'jouk'.

On the same day as he completed his masterpiece 'The Divine Comedy', the Italian poet Dante died.

The Chinese used fingerprints as a method of identification as far back as AD 700.

DECEMBER (24)

A large meteorite fell in Leicestershire on 24 December 1965. Weighing over one hundred pounds, it is probably the largest to have fallen in Britain in modern times.

Waves 'break' when their height is more than seven-tenths of the depth of the water.

American Red Indians used to name their children after the first thing they saw as they left their teepees subsequent to the birth. Hence such strange names as Sitting Bull, and Running Water.

It is a criminal offence to drive around in a dirty car in Russia.

It has been estimated that there are something like twenty-three million cats in the US.

DECEMBER (25)

The great film comedian, W.C. Fields, died on Christmas Day in 1946. His tombstone bore the following epitaph: 'On the whole I would rather be in Philadelphia.'

Vampire bats can hear sound frequencies which are over eight times higher than any picked up by the human ear.

Queen Elizabeth I passed a law which forced everyone except the rich to wear a flat cap on Sundays.

The warrior tribes of Ethiopia used to hang the testicles of those they killed in battle on the ends of their spears.

Spread out, the walls of the human intestines would cover an area of about one hundred square feet.

DECEMBER (26)

Mao Tse-Tung, the first Chairman of the Chinese Communist Party, was born today in 1893. Before his dizzy rise to power, he occupied the humble position of Assistant Librarian at the University of Peking.

There is a village near the Somme in France which is simply called Y.

In parts of Malaya, the women keep harems of men.

About half of the pianos in Britain are thought to be out of tune.

Football was banned in Tudor England because it was considered to be too rough.

DECEMBER (27)

Marlene Dietrich was born today in 1901. She was one of the most popular film actresses of her day, and was considered an expert on men. She once said: 'Most women set out to try to change a man, and when they have changed him they do not like him.'

About a quarter of the people bitten by dogs seem to be bitten by German shepherd dogs.

There are more living organisms on the skin of a single human being than there are human beings on the surface of the earth.

Widows in equatorial Africa actually wear sackcloth and ashes when attending a funeral.

The largest shark ever caught with a rod was just under seventeen feet long.

DECEMBER (28)

Maurice Ravel, the French composer, died on this day in 1937. He suffered from a debilitating brain disease late in his life, which left him unable to speak or even sign his own name.

Crocodiles are responsible for over a thousand deaths a year by the banks of the Nile.

Some very Orthodox Jews refuse to speak Hebrew, believing it to be a language reserved only for the Prophets.

After the first year, birthdays are usually celebrated only every ten years in China.

At full tilt, pumas can leap a distance of about sixty feet.

DECEMBER 29

The Liberal Prime Minister, William Gladstone, was born on 29 December 1809. Apparently, as a result of his strong Puritan impulses, Gladstone kept a selection of whips in his cellar with which he regularly chastised himself.

The women of the Tiwi tribe in the South Pacific are forced to marry at birth.

The Barbary apes in Gibraltar are well protected by the resident British. The tradition is that when the apes leave the Rock, the British will not be far behind.

Very hard rain would pour down at the rate of about twenty miles an hour.

The Tibetan mountain people use yaks' milk as their form of currency.

DECEMBER 30

The Russian mystic, Rasputin, was the victim of a series of murder attempts on this day in 1916. The assassins poisoned, shot, and stabbed him in quick succession, but they found they were unable to finish him off. Rasputin finally succumbed to the ice-cold waters of a river, but he certainly put up a fight.

Within a year of the implementation of Prohibition in America, the number of drinking places in New York more than doubled.

From the age of thirty, humans gradually begin to shrink in size.

A Flemish artist is responsible for one of the smallest paintings in history. It is a picture of a miller and his mill, and it was painted on to a grain of corn.

Some snakes can take as long as twenty-four hours to copulate.

DECEMBER (31)

'Bonnie Prince Charlie', the leader of the Jacobite rebellion to depose George II of England, was born today in 1720. Considered a great Scottish hero, he spent his final years as a drunkard in Rome.

For every extra pound carried on a space flight, 2,590 pounds of excess fuel are needed.

The Anglo-Saxons believed Friday to be such an unlucky day that they ritually slaughtered any child unfortunate enough to be born on it.

St Bernards, famous for their role as Alpine rescue dogs, do **not** wear casks of brandy round their necks.

Sharks' teeth are literally as hard as steel.

THE NATIONAL PLAYING FIELDS ASSOCIATION

Sixty years ago the National Playing Fields Association was established with a simple mandate: every child has a right to play. Nothing could be simpler. Yet our society is losing sight of this simple idea.

The NPFA has not, and is now one of the most effective voices for better play provision. It is not a fashionable cause. Nor is it an emotional cause. It is a cause concerned with the bed-rock on which our society is founded.

We live in a world designed and built for adults by adults. Children must live in this world too. It is the world in which they have to grow. A vital part of that growing-up process is play. For children, play is not trivial or unimportant. It is an integral part of their healthy development. It is in their play that children learn about life and about living — their preparation for their future. Without it, the deprived child develops into the deprived adult. Children need to play and have the right to grow and develop in freedom and in safety.

A concern for how children grow and develop is a concern for the future and the shape our society will take. The NPFA believes that we are failing our children, ourselves and our future in this key area. But it is still not too late, though the call for action grows more urgent.

We call our world 'the developed world'. How do children see it? They see: high rise flats; estates with postage-stamp gardens; signs which say 'Keep off the Grass' and 'No Ball Games Here'; more space for cars than for children. It is not just the environment which has become alien, almost hostile, to children, but people as well. We have separated children from adults in their work, their education and their leisure.

We are destroying their play world. We are placing our children at risk and in doing so we place our future at risk. The simple needs are often forgotten.

The Real Needs
In providing real play opportunities we can no longer salve our consciences by giving expensive toys and play equipment. Just to provide swings and roundabouts is only scratching at the surface of children's real needs. It is not just a question of space and equipment. Children also need:

> to be creative
> to be stimulated and challenged
> to be involved in all aspects of life.

Otherwise they will seek their excitement in other ways.

Most of all the NPFA believes children need people. Children need the care and involvement of adults in their play. This means nothing less than a total change of attitudes. Bringing children — and their play — into the centre of our lives and thinking.

When we plan for children we plan for our future. The NPFA believes this means fighting for children:

> fighting to give them space
> fighting to give them time to play
> fighting to give them opportunities for play
> fighting to involve people in their play

Above all else, the NPFA is fighting for the child's right to play. It means making the right choices in allocating our national resources. Play is cost effective:

> it saves — repairing children's bodies and minds
> it saves — by lessening delinquency, violence and vandalism
> it saves — by preventing stress in families.

That is what the NPFA's appeal for children's play is about. It is the only organization with the potential to fight effectively for children's play. We urgently need your help and support:

> to create a greater understanding of the value of play to children
> to persuade both public and private sectors of their responsibilities to children
> to improve the quantity and quality of play opportunities for children
> to support means of involving adults in the play — and therefore the lives of children
> to search for new initiatives for children's play provision.

In fact:
TO FIGHT FOR THE CHILD'S RIGHT TO PLAY.

If you would like to help, this is the address to write to:

The National Playing Fields Association,
25 Ovington Square,
London SW3 1LQ.
Telephone: 01-584 6445.